*The author wishes to acknowledge the
help and advice given by his colleagues
in the trade and especially;*

*Mr. Adrian Bloom, author of the
previous book in this series 'Conifers For
Your Garden',*

*Mr. D. John Sales, N.D.H.,
nationally known gardens advisor,*

*The staff of the Writtle College of
Agriculture whose planting schemes are
shown among the black and white
photographs, and Mr. Michael Warren
for his excellent photographs.*

FRONT COVER:
Chaenomeles x superba 'Crimson and Gold'

INSIDE FRONT COVER:
A narrow border planted with *Pyracantha*
and other shrubs to screen an unsightly
concrete garage in the author's garden.

INSIDE BACK COVER:
Viburnum plicatum 'Lanarth' (left) and
Philadelphus coronarius 'Aureus' (right)

BACK COVER:
Lonicera periclymenum, the "Common Honeysuckle"

SHRUBS
FOR YOUR
GARDEN

by Peter Seabrook

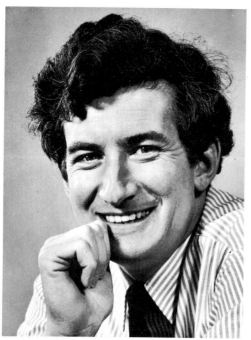

Peter Seabrook

If any one person in England deserved the title "Mr. Horticulture" Peter Seabrook should be that person.

While still in his 30's he has spent more than 20 years in the garden world. He gained the National Diploma of Horticulture following training at Writtle College near Chelmsford and then spent more than 10 years with Cramphorn the well known Chelmsford Company, who have Nurseries, Garden Centres and Shops throughout the South East of England. He was one of the leading lights in the forming of the British Group of the International Garden Centre Association and through his experience as their first Field Officer gained first hand knowledge of the English gardening public, their likes and dislikes. His knowledge and experience in the relatively modern field of Garden Centres is second to none.

Although this is his first complete book Peter Seabrook writes regularly for many of the horticultural magazines, both amateur and professional. With his particular knowledge of the modern gardening scene and his background experience of nursery shrub production he is more than qualified to write on shrubs for gardens.

It is knowledge of shrubs coupled with his perception of what the modern gardener needs that makes 'Shrubs for your Garden' so useful a book.

Floraprint books are published by Burrall + Floraprint Ltd., Wisbech.

ISBN 0 903001 03 9.

First published 1973 by Floraprint Ltd., Calverton.
Reprinted 1974, 1979, 1980, 1983, 1985, 1987.

Printed in France.

Shrubs for your garden

Easily grown woody perennial plants, ranging from 20 cm low shrubs to small trees are available in a tremendous range of form, colour and fragrance. There are types to suit every situation, both formal garden layouts and natural settings. No patch of soil is either too large or too small to accommodate examples of these popular plants. Indeed even the smallest patio or yard can be improved by using shrubs in containers such as tubs and troughs. Suitable varieties can be found for every site and soil type.

Evergreen and deciduous shrubs, low, medium and tall growing, provide a contrast in form and colour right through the year. Note the ground covering, weed smothering effect of Potentilla, Erica and Hypericum to the front of the border.

EVERGREEN AND DECIDUOUS SHRUBS

While the selection of shrubs will vary widely with each person's likes and dislikes, most collections will contain both evergreen and deciduous subjects. The evergreens, by holding their foliage the year round, have obvious advantages for screening, furnishing the garden in winter, deflecting noise and filtering wind to provide shelter. In contrast deciduous plants have bare branches throughout the dormant season but more than compensate for this with their fresh new growth in spring followed by the verdant canopy in summer and the kaleidoscope of autumn colour before leaf fall.

Foliage is but one of the effects provided: equally important are the beauty and interest of bark and twigs and the colour and fragrance of flowers and fruits. All the attributes of each shrub need consideration when forming a collection and planning a scheme of planting.

The coloured barks and unusual form taken by the branches of some shrubs are worthy of greater attention, especially to add interest to the garden in winter. The brilliant scarlet of *Cornus* and willow bark and the tortured twisting of the hazel are excellent examples. Thought should be given to the background for such plants; dark evergreens contrast the brightly coloured barks; silver or golden evergreens are a way of highlighting corkscrewed and twisted branches.

Fragrance is considered in two forms: the heady air-filled fragrance of the more strongly scented like *Philadelphus*, honeysuckle and *Azalea mollis*, and the more subtle perfumes requiring special knowledge and more personal attention to savour and appreciate. Examples of the latter include the need to crush rosemary leaves between the fingers, to bruise the sage varieties and move to visit sweetbriars after rain.

Whilst quantity and brightness of colour are the obvious qualities required from the fruit, two less obvious but equally important points are, the length of time the fruits remain on the plant and their attractiveness to birds. Of the flowering and fruiting crabs, the well known 'John Downie' will ripen and fall long before 'Golden Hornet', a cultivar whose abundance of freely-produced fruits are held well past Christmas. The orange and yellow-berried *Pyracanthas* appear to be less attractive to birds than the red and the large fruits of *Chaenomeles* usually remain throughout the winter. Plants like the *Malus* 'John Downie' are better planted in such a way that their branches do not overhang paths because the ripe fallen fruit can be messy and quite dangerous when trodden underfoot.

Water is a feature of gardens which helps to develop the third dimension by reflection. Species of *Cornus* and willow are commonly found in this situation but smaller and more profuse flowering shrubs can double their glory with a reflected image. The reflection of clear blue summer skies and effervescent white *Viburnum* is a striking example.

The gardener is faced with a choice when purchasing shrubs, from the left a balled plant, a bare-root plant and a container grown plant. The bare roots of plants lifted from the open ground must not be allowed to dry out during the period from lifting to replanting.

SIZE AND GROWTH

Speed of growth and eventual height and spread will vary according to district, soil and situation. The vital statistics listed in this book are the averages reached under normal garden conditions. It should be remembered that plants growing in shade may be drawn up, that warm positions, high rainfall and rich soils will speed growth and can increase ultimate size. Equally, cold and dry positions and impoverished soil will restrict the size and speed of growth.

Bright sunlight, therefore south facing slopes will provide the brightest coloured leaves of silver and golden variegated plants. Shady sites and rich soils, high in nitrogen, are likely to reduce the brightness of variegation.

When the ultimate heights are known, mixed groups can be planted in such a way that they grow in balance one with another. Like an artist using colour, each selected plant is used to build the complete but everchanging picture. This is the enthralling part of gardening: a continual challenge offering something of beauty and interest every day. If small plants are used at the outset, groups of each can be planted for quick effect and thinned as they increase in size and require more space.

Vigorous young plants will often establish themselves after transplanting more quickly than larger specimens that suffer a more severe check when moved. Furthermore, young plants retain the vigour of youth, often growing away fast enough to overtake larger plants of the same kind. This fact needs bearing in mind when a large area of new garden is to be planted and economics are a serious consideration.

Groups of three, five and larger odd numbers are preferred, a single plant being left perhaps to remain as the final specimen when thinning has been completed. Compared with the cost of building and site preparation and labour costs in maintenance, plants are a small part of the total cost of a garden layout. The use of increased numbers will provide a much faster achievement of the mature appearance. Three plants, to be thinned to one finally, may well cover the ground in a season and save two whole seasons of fortnightly hoeing for weed control where only one plant was used from the outset.

Trees on a clear stem give height. Taller and upright growing shrubs can be used to the centre and back of any planting, weeping and trailing forms over walls and on banks.

Ground-hugging prostrate plants can be used to cover the ground beneath larger specimens. A number of evergreens are described which can be used in this way. These ground covers are attractive in their own right but additionally they make gardening easy by smothering weeds and ultimately require very little maintenance.

The introduction of "container growing" has revolutionised shrub gardening and, with a good supply of pot grown plants, transplanting can be undertaken at any time of the year. We now have the three options open to us:

1. Bare root plants, lifted from the field and transported free of soil. The roots are wrapped with material to keep them moist.

2. Balled plants, lifted from the field with the soil ball around the roots held firmly in place. Burlap or hessian (open-weave material like sacking) holds the soil in place and allows transplanting with the minimum of root disturbance.

3. Container plants, grown in pots, can be transplanted at any time in the year with no root disturbance and no check to the plant.

Container and balled plants are heavy and as a result mail order carriage charges are expensive. For this reason it is cheaper to purchase from a local nursery or garden centre. The garden centre also allows for personal choice of well shaped, vigorously growing specimens. Where less common plants are required, orders should be placed with reputable specialist companies.

Cheap offers and low priced plants are all too often either inferior varieties or starved, checked, very young or diseased plants, that may eventually prove to be a bad buy. The fair price of really good plants is an investment, which every year grows in value.

All the plants illustrated and described are available in the United Kingdom, most of them from the better retail nurseries and garden centres. Improved and recently introduced varieties of merit are listed and these are well worth seeking out. Some are not yet available in great numbers and for these it is well worth making a reservation early in the season, to avoid disappointment.

It should be remembered that plants, like human beings, are doing their utmost to live and grow. Good, healthy plants will thrive with remarkably little attention, whilst improving our environment and giving endless pleasure. In the continual search for better photographs to illustrate the plants now available, I am constantly reminded that perfect specimens are to be found even in the smallest suburban garden.

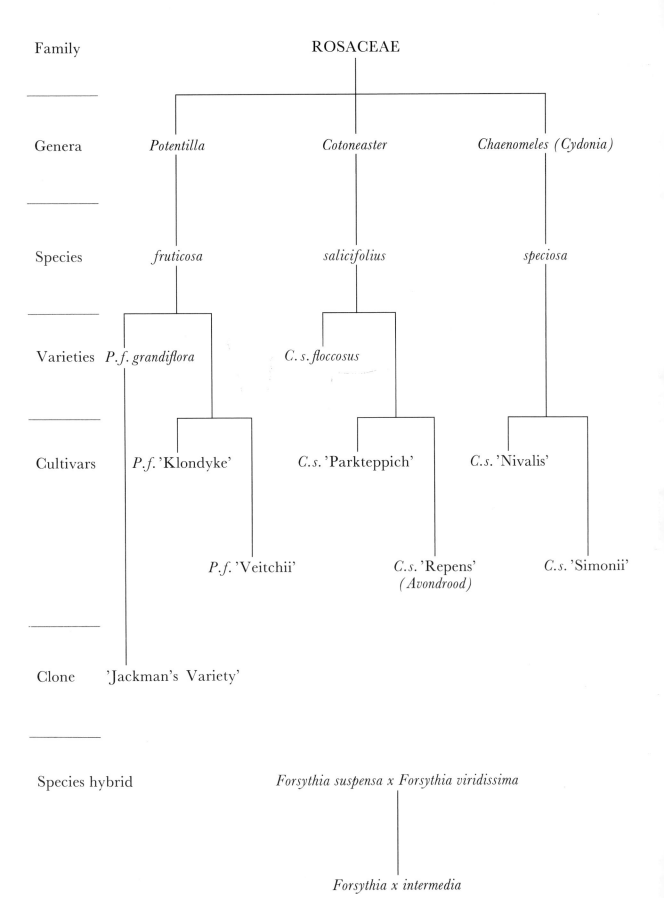

Family   ROSACEAE

Genera   *Potentilla*   *Cotoneaster*   *Chaenomeles (Cydonia)*

Species   *fruticosa*   *salicifolius*   *speciosa*

Varieties *P.f. grandiflora*   *C. s. floccosus*

Cultivars   *P.f.* 'Klondyke'   *C.s.* 'Parkteppich'   *C.s.* 'Nivalis'

                              P.f. 'Veitchii'   *C.s.* 'Repens'   *C.s.* 'Simonii'
                                                    (Avondrood)

Clone   'Jackman's Variety'

Species hybrid   *Forsythia suspensa x Forsythia viridissima*

                              Forsythia x intermedia

7

NAMING OF SHRUBS

The long Latin names of plants are a frightening obstacle to the gardening newcomer and too many of us create a complete and yet quite unnecessary mental blockage from the start. This is a great pity because these names are useful in breaking language barriers and in providing information about the plant, once a few simple terms are understood.

From the tongue-twisting name *Acer palmatum* 'Dissectum Atropurpureum', one of the maples, we can decipher that the leaves are palm shaped (palmatum), finely cut (Dissectum) and deep purple in colour. It is easy to get to know the terms and before long the meanings of words like *praecox*—early flowering—will be remembered. A catalogue of plant names provides a considerable amount of information about the plants. Leaf shape, size and colour, flower form and size of plants are but some of the qualities included in shrub names.

Common names in the native tongue, whilst instantly appealing, create confusion. In some cases one name is applied to two or more quite different plants by people in different localities. Additionally, newly introduced plants will have no common name. To avoid confusion all gardeners and nurserymen need to use the same name. There is nothing more disheartening than to cultivate a desired plant only to find on flowering and fruiting that it is not what was wanted. Even worse is the purchase of two allegedly different plants to find that they differ only in name.

Shrubs are classified by botanists, in the same way as all other plants, according to flower type into large groups called families. The family name is not likely to be of any great importance to gardeners and is not included in the title by which we refer to each kind.

Genera, the plural of genus, refers to the first names, almost the surnames, of our garden shrubs. Every genus contains one or more species and all plants within the genus have basic characteristics in common. Well known examples of genera include *Cotoneaster, Forsythia, Hydrangea, Magnolia* and *Potentilla*.

Species. Plants having more characteristics in common that the genera, occurring naturally and interbreeding freely, are known as species. Examples of well known *Cotoneaster* species are: *C. conspicuus, C. dammeri, C. horizontalis, C. microphyllus, C. salicifolius, C. simonsii* and *C. wardii*. All have an abundance of white or pink tinged flowers in early summer and attractive berries in autumn and winter.

Varieties. Species are variable in the wild some to the point that they are distinct enough to be regarded separately as varieties. Examples of this include *C. dammeri radicans, C. horizontalis perpusillus* and *C. microphyllus thymifolius*. The latter illustrates further the value of the Latin, as it will be seen that when translated this variety has narrow, thyme-like leaves.

Cultivars. This term is normally used to describe plants which have arisen in cultivation usually as hybrids, sports and chance seedlings. The term also embraces plants which have been specially selected in the wild for their distinctive shape, form or colour and which are maintained in cultivation by vegetative propagation. The cultivar name is normally written in single quotation marks, for example 'Autumn Fire', 'Fructu-luteo', 'Parkteppich' and 'Repens'; all of these are cultivars of *Cotoneaster salicifolius*.

Clone. This is the term applied to a group of plants derived originally from a single unique specimen and increased by vegetative propagation. All plants of a single clone are exactly alike and identical with the original. It will be seen that most vegetatively propagated shrub cultivars are clonal. The term clonal is likely to be used more in the future now that modern scientific methods for eliminating virus diseases are being employed to "clean up" old cultivars. Better growth has already been obtained from mother plants of *Prunus* (flowering cherries) and *Malus* (flowering crabs), which have been freed of viruses.

Hybrid. When a plant has been produced by the crossing of two genera or species, the Latin name is correctly preceeded by a cross. For example, *Forsythia x intermedia* is the result of a cross between two *Forsythia* species *F. suspensa* and *F. viridissima*.

There remains one further point of explanation: the change of plant names under the "Rule of Priority". It has been agreed by botanists that the earliest recorded name will be legitimate and with continuous historic research taking place many changes are made. One of the more recent changes, that illustrates this point, is the well known winter flowering shrub *Viburnum fragrans*, now correctly known as *V. farreri*.

Where they are generally accepted, correct botanical names are used in this book, in some cases with the old synonym following in brackets.

8

The many uses of shrubs

For many people shrubbery conjures up dense, woody growth two to three metres high, overcrowded, dark and far from attractive. It is not until we stop to think about the value of shrubs in gardens that their adaptable nature and useful role is fully appreciated.

Dowdy and dusty old shrubberies are too common because planting has been done carelessly, without the all important time spent on planning, that is choosing the right kinds for the right place and space. These errors at the outset are made worse by neglecting even the small amount of attention that shrubs require.

For a mixed shrub border your selection could include all the qualities that shrubs possess. Low growing and ground covering plants would be used at the front of the border, taller shrubs at the back. Evergreens and attractive bark furnish the garden in winter. Your choice could include a succession of flowers throughout the year or selections to give attractive features in spring or autumn.

Quite apart from the accepted role in borders, as an attractive feature in their own right, and in beds to provide protection, privacy and a pleasant vista, shrubs are adaptable to many garden uses. We have the many climbing and clinging plants that are excellent on fences and for screening, the varieties which tolerate clipping to form hedges and informal barriers, shrubs suited to restricted root growth for troughs and tubs, as well as wall plants and ground cover subjects.

There are countless varieties to choose from and, as can be seen from the illustrations in this book, many of them are of outstanding beauty.

Here is the low growing Hebe pinguifolia 'Pagei' in full flower against a backcloth of mixed Berberis and Cotoneaster in a small border. The tree gives height to the planting scheme.

Shrubs for ground cover are gaining in popularity. Here Cotoneaster horizontalis, foreground, and Cotoneaster dammeri are used to carpet the soil and reduce maintenance to the minimum. Taller shrubs and trees are used to give height and to screen the back of the border.

One of the author's favourite plants, Clematis montana is an excellent example of plants for screening. It will tolerate any aspect, even north and quickly covers an unsightly fence or building with vigorous growth.

A brick trough less than 1 metre square comfortably accommodates this plant of Genista hispanica. It produces masses of yellow flowers in May and June and protects itself with small gorse-like thorns.

Plants for patios can include species which prefer hot, dry, well drained soils, like the Yucca, and the more tender plants, like the fragrant Choisya ternata (Left).

Many shrubs respond to regular trimming and grow either into formal hedges or, with less hard and less frequent cutting, into informal screens.

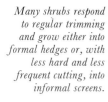

Many shrubs are suited to furnishing walls. The Cotoneaster horizontalis shown here is a good example.

Shrubs selected for special purposes

FOR FRAGRANCE

Choisya ternata
Daphne mezereum
Jasminum officinale
Mahonia 'Charity'
Philadelphus 'Virginal'
Syringa vulgaris cultivars

FOR GROUND COVER

Cotoneaster, for example *dammeri*
Cytisus x kewensis
Euonymus radicans cultivars
Hebe rakaiensis (syn. *subalpina*)
Hedera species
Hypericum calycinum
Prunus laurocerasus 'Otto Luyken'

FOR AUTUMN COLOUR

Amelanchier canadensis
Euonymus europaeus
Leycesteria formosa
Rhus typhina
Ribes odoratum
Viburnum opulus

FOR WINTER FLOWERS

Chimonanthus praecox
Cornus mas
Erica carnea
Garrya elliptica
Hamamelis mollis
Viburnum farreri

FOR BERRIES AND FRUITS

Callicarpa bodinieri
Chaenomeles speciosa
Hippophae rhamnoides
Malus species
Pyracantha
Rosa moyesii
Skimmia japonica

FOR STEEP BANKS

Cotoneaster, for example 'Skogholm'
Cytisus praecox
Lavandula spica
Potentilla fruticosa
Spiraea x bumalda
Vinca major 'Variegata'

FOR HOT DRY SITES

Berberis species
Caryopteris x clandonensis
Genista hispanica
Perovskia atriplicifolia
Senecio greyi
Spartium junceum

FOR SHADE

Aucuba japonica
Euonymus radicans cultivars
Hydrangea petiolaris
Ilex species
Mahonia aquifolium
Rhododendron
Viburnum tinus

Mixed shrubs, predominantly evergreen, give attractive cover to this hot bank at the foot of a low wall. Some judicial pruning back will be required to contain the growth of Cotoneaster.

Seedheads on the Clematis are attractive in winter, extending the season of beauty of this climbing and screening plant.

Closely planted low growing shrubs can be attractive all the year round and require very little maintenance. Prunus laurocerasus 'Otto Luyken' in the foreground is an excellent example.

Soil preparation and planting shrubs

Plants will cling desperately to life despite unsatisfactory conditions. It is worth remembering that, with just a little help, shrubs will not only live but flourish and grow with vigour. They will thrive in virtually all garden soils: the only qualification being to select the kinds carefully where extremes of alkalinity (chalk), acidity (peat and thin sands) and bad drainage occur.

All perennial plants require a soil which has been well prepared by cultivation and manuring. If the preparation has been carried out thoroughly the life of the planting scheme will be lengthened, the maintenance of the border made easier and the results will be more satisfying. Firstly, shrubs and plants with woody growth require at least thirty centimetres of well dug soil to accommodate the roots. Quick establishment and rapid growth will be achieved where there is ample depth of soil for free root growth. For this reason the soil should be cultivated two spits, that is two spades, deep.

Whilst to double dig the whole site is the ideal treatment, for most practical purposes digging the top spit thoroughly and forking through the lower spit at the same time will suffice. All perennial weeds should be removed during the preparatory digging. Both light and heavy soils are greatly improved by the incorporation of peat and well rotted compost.

Plant nutrients in the form of fertilisers are easily applied in subsequent seasons but after planting there is little chance of improving the soil structure. It is not by chance that peat is used in increasing quantities by the present-day gardener, because most soils are quickly, and quite dramatically, improved if sufficient peat is thoroughly incorporated during the initial cultivations. I recommend the light coloured sphagnum peats provided that they are well moistened before incorporation.

After cultivation, the site is best left for a period to settle before planting the shrubs. Where it is necessary to plant into newly dug soil, firming by trampling may well be necessary after digging. In many cases the shrub border will be surrounded by lawns and here a planting sheet, to carry spare soil whilst digging the planting hole and then refilling, will protect the grass and give a clean finish to the job.

A hole large enough to accommodate fully the shrub roots is required. Be sure to keep bare roots protected from cold and drying winds during preparation for planting. A damp sack or cloth will be adequate for this. When the shrub is in position, good friable soil enriched with damp peat is filled in around the roots. Bare-rooted shrubs should be eased up and down gently at the start of infilling to ensure that the soil comes into close contact with the roots and that no large air pockets remain.

As the filling in progresses, so the soil is firmed by treading. Once this is complete, the footmarks should be forked out. Where footprints are left to remain after planting, the structure of the soil will be damaged by becoming wet and sticky and drying into a hard cake. Soil structure, that lovely, easy-to-work, crumbly nature of good soil, is also damaged by planting during wet conditions. When the soil is very wet, planting is better delayed, especially on heavy soils. Planting should also be delayed when the ground is frozen.

Dig a hole large enough to accommodate the roots.

Fill in with friable soil.

...and firm as you go.

A hole large enough for a container grown plant.

Place in position and remove the container.

Firm well and then fork out the footprints.

Hedge plant positioned...

Ensure the soil is firmed around the roots

Prune back by half after planting.

CONTAINER PLANTS

Well grown container plants are the easiest to handle because in prepared soil we only need a hole fractionally larger than the container. Make sure that the plant is established in the container before purchasing it. Well established plants can be lifted by the stem and will hold the full weight of pot and compost. Recently potted subjects are best left with the nurseryman and garden centre until fully established. Once the hole has been made, place the plant in position, *remove* the container, and fill in with fine soil: then firm. It is acceptable to leave the sacking-like hessian material around balled plants, because this quickly decays. All other containers, which might restrict root growth and cause drying out of the soil ball, are better removed.

DELIVERY DURING BAD WEATHER

Container plants will not come to any harm if planting is delayed, as long as they are not allowed to dry out. Bare-rooted plants should be left in the wrapping, free from frost and kept damp. When the plants arrive prior to site preparation, they can be temporarily "laid in", that is the roots placed in a trench on vacant ground, covered with moist soil and firmed.

HEDGES AND LIVING SCREENS

Patience is the key to success with hedges, especially in the first year or two after planting. Once again I cannot stress too strongly the value of digging the soil well and adding plenty of peat, well rotted compost and similar organic matter. If you want a real living screen then vigorous, well branched growth has to be supported for many years and while top dressing with fertiliser and watering this in during dry weather will help to sustain growth there is no substitute for a well prepared foundation at the outset.

The planting sequence is not different to the sequence for shrubs. Where a long row has to be planted, take the soil from the first hole right down the line to the last site. The soil for the second hole can then be used to plant the first specimen, the soil from the third to plant the second, and so on right down the row.

Where balled specimens are used of such good evergreens as "Laurel", *Berberis stenophylla*, "Yew" and "Holly" transplanting is best done in September/October and March/April. All bare root plants will need to be transplanted at any time during the dormant season from October to March as long as the soil is free of frost. Container plants can, of course, be transplanted at any time. Be sure to keep them well watered during dry weather, especially strong growing subjects like "Flowering Currant", "Privet" and "Laurel". Given this treatment they will establish themselves very quickly and soon provide the desired screening effect.

PRUNING

The first year after planting the important thing is to develop plenty of basal shoots to furnish the hedge and screen right to the base. Planting a double row of the cheaper plants like "Privet", "Quickthorn" and "Seedling Beech" will help provide a very dense screen. All the deciduous subjects planted bare root should be cut back by half before the end of the spring following planting. It may break your heart to lose the height, especially if a quick screen is wanted, but pruning back the first year will, in the long run, prove very worthwhile. One other useful tip is to plant strong growing plants like "Seedling Beech" and "Quickthorn" at a 45° angle. The shoots then grow along the stem rather than from the tip and this again increases the number of basal shoots.

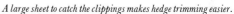

A large sheet to catch the clippings makes hedge trimming easier.

Pruning

Most shrubs need very little pruning. In terms of general garden care, it should be a case of retaining their shape and proportion and removing dead heads after flowering. Be sure to have a good sharp pair of secateurs, both for the sake of the plant and for your own comfort. It is easier to remove a large branch if, when the cut is made, pressure is applied downwards and away from the blade, on the piece of shrub to be removed.

Pruning can be classified into four fairly clearly defined groups, one for evergreens and three for deciduous shrubs.

EVERGREENS

Recently transplanted specimens, which would have had considerable root disturbance, require their leading shoots, the strongest growing branches, to be cut back by one half. Balled and container-grown plants, which would have had a minimum of root disturbance, and established plants require no more than the removal of weak, straggly and diseased shoots. Evergreens pruned in April quickly produce new growth to hide any unsightly cut stumps. A few plants like *Buxus, Lavandula, Olearia, Rhododendron* and *Santolina* respond to hard pruning and, where they are bare at the base and have outgrown their site, they can be cut back in spring.

DECIDUOUS

Spring flowering shrubs

The deciduous kinds, which flower in spring and early summer, for example *Ribes, Forsythia, Philadelphus* and *Syringa,* are pruned immediately after flowering. The old, flowered shoots should be cut back to fresh young growths on the main branches. Weak growth should be removed and crowded shoots thinned out at this time.

Summer flowering shrubs

Late summer and early antumn flowering shrubs, which flower on the current year's growth, are best pruned hard, in early spring. Plants like *Buddleia davidii* cultivars, *Caryopteris, Fuchsia, Hibiscus, Potentilla* and *Tamarix pentandra* will respond well to this hard annual pruning.

Good, clean cuts are soon covered with strong new growth. The Buddleia here responds well to hard spring pruning.

Winter flowering shrubs

Weak, diseased and straggling branches are best removed during the spring. Pruning to keep them within a restricted space is all that is additionally required.

PESTS AND DISEASES

Fortunately this subject is a minor one in the cultivation of shrubs. Except for aphis on plants like cherries and crabs, pests and diseases common to a range of shrubs are few and are rarely experienced generally. Specific parasites like rhododendron Leafhopper are mentioned under the plant headings.

Scale insects, which are usually found on the underside of leaves and against the main leaf veins, can be troublesome on a range of plants. Control can be achieved on deciduous plants with tar oil in December and January. This will also clean up moss, lichen and algae growth. Tar oil must *not* be used on some plants, for example evergreens, *Pyracantha* and deciduous *Azaleas.* Control of scale on evergreens like *Camellia* can be obtained by repeated spraying with Malathion in July and August.

Opposite page :
This colourful planting scheme has Spiraea x bumalda 'Anthony Waterer' *in the foreground,* Cornus alba 'Elegantissima' *to the left and* Cotinus coggygria.

Beds planted with one kind of shrub are a feature in the garden which is easily maintained. The evergreen Berberis x stenophylla and Syringa vulgaris cultivars are excellent examples.

ABELIA

These summer and autumn flowering shrubs are deciduous, semi-evergreen and evergreen, and deserve much wider use.

They flower over a long period and are easy to grow, even in cold districts, given the protection of a south facing wall. Most species require such protection in all but the warmer southern and western parts of the country.

Throughout the flowering season, many clusters of tubular flowers festoon the tips of branches and side-shoots. Attractive, mid to dark green, ovate leaves are an excellent foil to the flowers and are attractive in their own right for the rest of the year.

Light, loamy soils are best but any open, free draining soil will produce satisfactory growth. Pruning is no more demanding then the removal of old and dead wood after flowering, together with trimming to retain the desired shape. The smaller, scented species are ideal for planting close to the house and in the corners of patios and terraces.

Three species are usually grown in shrub nurseries and all are worthwhile garden varieties.

Abelia x grandiflora is semi evergreen, growing 1.5 m. in height and spread. The pink and white flowers are produced from July to September. *Abelia schumanii* is of similar size with lilac-pink flowers from June to September. It may often be cut back by frost but shoots again from ground level in spring.

Abelia triflora is upright and grows more vigorously, eventually to 3.5 m. high. White flowers tinged pink, with a heavenly scent, are produced, as the name suggests, in threes during June.

Abelia x grandiflora

19

ACER
Maple

type

'Variegatum'

'Elegans'

A. negundo leaf detail

Acer negundo 'Variegatum'

One of the most popular of genera is the *Acer*, commonly referred to as "Maple", which ranges from dwarf and slow growing shrubs to large and stately trees. There are two clear groups which can be classified as small trees and shrubs, the "Box Elders", *Acer negundo*, and the "Japanese Maples", *Acer palmatum*.

All are quite hardy, deciduous, and have attractive foliage and bark, but not flowers. Japanese types are lime tolerant but grow best in moist, well drained soils that are either slightly acid or have been enriched with peat. The varieties with finely cut and attractively coloured leaves are damaged by late spring frosts and strong winds. For this reason they should, if possible, be planted in sites sheltered both from direct early morning sunshine and prevailing winds.

Acer negundo can be grown either as a tall shrub or as a bushy-headed tree. Both the foliage and the young wood of the type are bright green and it grows to 8 m. in height and 5–6 m. spread. The smaller forms with variegated leaves are used extensively in gardens, both as shrubs, with branches breaking from ground level, and as trees on a short trunk or "leg".

Acer negundo 'Variegatum' (syn. 'Argenteovariegateum') has broad white margins to the leaves.

Acer negundo 'Elegans' (syn. 'Elegantissimum') has bright yellow variegation.

The two variegated cultivars are good small trees to grow in pots and tubs. They are also attractive when planted in association with the purple leaved *Prunus*.

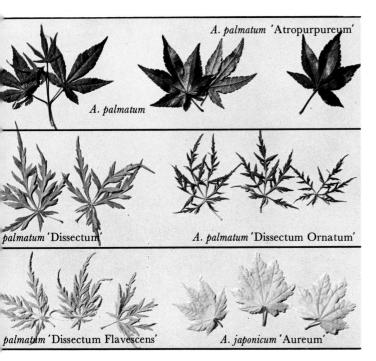

A. palmatum 'Atropurpureum'

A. palmatum

palmatum 'Dissectum'

A. palmatum 'Dissectum Ornatum'

palmatum 'Dissectum Flavescens'

A. japonicum 'Aureum'

Acer palmatum 'Dissectum'

Acer palmatum 'Dissectum Atropurpureum'

Most popular *Acer palmatum* forms have delicate, deeply-cut leaves and a slow-growing rounded habit, which is ideal for smaller gardens. The changing leaf colour in autumn is quite startling and includes all shades of red, orange and yellow.

The most commonly planted is *Acer palmatum* 'Atropurpureum', which has striking dark bronze leaves and grows eventually to 4–5 m. high. *Acer palmatum* 'Dissectum' has very deeply cut and finely divided leaves. It is so slow growing that it may reach little more than 1 m. in ten years. As well as the green cultivar 'Dissectum' there are others which include *A. p.* 'Dissectum Flavescens', pale yellow green, *A. p.* 'Dissectum Ornatum', pale bronze and *A. p.* 'Dissectum Atropurpureum', deep purple.

Acer japonicum 'Aureum' is similar in size to the *Acer palmatum* 'Dissectum' cultivars and requires similar treatment. The attractive soft yellow leaves will scorch in full sun.

All the low growing shrubby *Acers* associate well with *Azaleas* and appreciate the protection and semi-shade of light woodland. The cut-leaved forms are suited to banks, specimen planting in grass and association with stone. A good combination is to plant lilies amongst Japanese *Acers. (Continued overleaf)*

The slow-growing *Acer pseudoplatanus* 'Brilliantissimum', although correctly classified as a small tree, can be grown on a short stem as a shrub. The leaves in spring open shrimp pink, and turn, as they mature, to pale yellow and finally green.

Acer pseudoplatanus 'Brilliantissimum'

AMELANCHIER

The Snowy Mespilus is a large shrub or small tree which should be much more widely planted in gardens and leisure areas. The young foliage is pink to copper coloured which contrasts in spring with clustered masses of whites flowers. The leaves are at their best, however, in the autumn, when they take on their soft autumnal hues of red and yellow. The small, scarlet, rounded fruits turn purple and sweet tasting when ripe. They are then very popular with blackbirds. Both open and partially shaded sites are suitable but the plant prefers moist conditions and a neutral to lime-free soil. Plants can be pruned back hard after flowering to keep them down to garden size. The *Amelanchiers* are excellent plants to use in association with spring bulbs. They can also be placed at the back of mixed shrubberies and used for screening.

Amelanchier canadensis is the most widely listed species and it can be increased by pulling away the suckers that grow out from the base of the plants. It grows up to 6 m. high and 2–3 m. across. The young leaves are woolly on both sides and this characteristic differentiates it from *A. laevis*, which is planted in many British gardens and incorrectly named *A. canadensis*. The leaves of *A. laevis* are especially colourful in the autumn.

Amelanchier canadensis

ARALIA

Aralia elata

Aralia elata 'Aureovariegata' with *Hedera* ground cover

Leaves giving a tropical effect are the most attractive feature of the genus *Aralia*, also known as the "Chinese and Japanese Angelica Trees". These hardy plants take on their tree-like proportions, up to 10 m. high, in the warmer parts of the country. They also succeed in cooler areas but with a shrubby habit with suckers being produced from the base of the plant.

Huge leaves up to 1.5 m. long radiate from the young shoots to provide a platform for the large clusters of small white flowers in August and September. *Aralia elata* is the most widely grown and two variegated cultivars are especially attractive. *Aralia elata* 'Aureo variegata' has both marginal and blotchy yellow markings on the leaves, whilst *A. e.* 'Variegata' has creamy-white variegation. Both become silvery white as the season advances. They are propagated by grafting and, because suitable grafting material does not grow freely, may not be obtained easily. *Aralia chinensis*, the Chinese Angelica differs from *A. elata* in having less spines and a longer flower stem.

AUCUBA JAPONICA

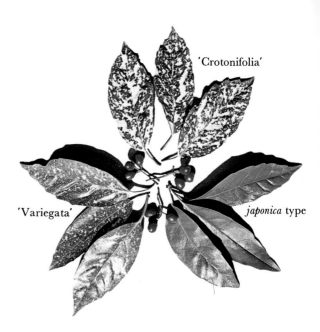

'Crotonifolia'

'Variegata'

japonica type

An excellent town plant, this versatile evergreen shrub will withstand dense shade and the dusty deposits of city life and smoky atmospheres. It is most attractive, however, when growing strongly in clean conditions; the rich glossy foliage becoming a feature. This is especially the case with variegated forms, which retain their colour longest when grown in full sun. Male and female flowers appear on separate plants and the latter, if cross pollinated, produce bright scarlet berries.

The capacity of this plant to withstand competition both for sunlight and for moisture is surprising. It has few equals for planting under trees, even in the dense shade of limes and beeches.

Almost any soil and situation is acceptable and pruning to limit size and retain shape should be undertaken in May and June. In addition to its use under trees, in borders and in mixed shrubberies, the *Aucuba* can be grown in tubs, urns and as a house plant. *Aucuba japonica* has glossy, dark green leaves and grows to 1.5 m. in height and spread. *A. j.* 'Crotonifolia' is a male plant and the best golden variegated form. *A. j.* 'Variegata' is a female variety with speckled yellow leaves.

Aucuba japonica 'Crotonifolia'

AZALEA

Azalea mollis in a range of colours.

Botanically *Azalea* is now placed under the generic heading *Rhododendron*.
In general garden terms, however, the two are still considered separately and,
for this reason, they are treated here as a separate section.
The taller growing kinds lose their leaves in autumn whilst the low growing types
are virtually evergreen.

Azalea 'Fedora'

Azalea 'Blue Danube'

Azalea 'Nancy Waterer'

Brilliantly coloured flowers, autumn foliage colour and fragrance are provided by *Azaleas*. They may be described as ideal garden plants, with both compact dwarf types and larger growing forms. Although they all require lime-free soil, it is possible to grow them in strongly alkaline conditions by making up raised beds of acid soil. Slightly alkaline soils are also suitable, provided that they are very generously enriched with acid peat. Care must be taken to ensure that alkaline water does not drain from surrounding soil into the specially prepared beds. An annual mulch of peat suits these surface rooting plants and encourages well balanced growth.

Evergreen *Azaleas*.

The evergreen and semi evergreen types include Kurume, Kaempferi and Vuyk hybrids and are generally described as Japanese *Azaleas*. These plants are quite hardy but early autumn and late spring frosts can sometimes damage the flower buds and young growth. Some of the flowers fade badly in strong sunlight. For these reasons, shelter from early morning sun and some shade is an advantage.

These compact shrubs may take ten years to reach 1 m. high and 1 m. across. Most cultivars are single flowered although new clones are being introduced which are double, semi-double and exhibit the "hose-in-hose" character, that is one single flower inside another to produce a double effect. Classification of the evergreens is usually by flower size. Recommended small flowered varieties, 2.5 to 3.5 cm. across, include 'Blue Danube', 'Hino-Crimson', 'Hino-Scarlet', 'Orange Beauty', 'Perfect', which is salmon pink and 'Rose Bud', clear pink. Large flowered varieties, 5 to 7.5 cm. across, include 'Double Beauty', fully double carmine rose, 'Fedora' pale pink; 'Florida' orange-red; 'Mothers Day' rose-red semi-double; 'Palestrina' white with a shadow of green; 'Vuyk's Rosy Red' and 'Vuyk's Scarlet'. All flower in April and May.

Azalea 'Hino-Mayo'

Azalea 'Coccinea Speciosa'

Deciduous *Azaleas*

This heading includes the Mollis, Ghent Hybrids and Knap Hill Hybrids, the latter being further developed to produce the Exbury Azaleas. They are deciduous plants and grow 1.5 to 2.5 m. in height although some varieties exceed this, especially under shaded conditions. Continued hybridisation tends to blur the distinctions between groups. The Ghent Hybrids are the tallest and have smaller, more tubular flowers with a strong fragrance. The Knap Hill and Mollis types have large flowers carried in bold trusses. They range in colour from white and pale cream to yellow, orange, flame, tangerine and pink.

Examples of well proven cultivars within each group are: *Exbury* 'Cecile', salmon pink; *Ghent* 'Coccinea Speciosa', brilliant orange red; 'Nancy Waterer', golden yellow; and *Mollis* 'Koster's Brilliant Red'. Numerous named cultivars are now listed in catalogues but the cheaper, unnamed seedlings, offered as mixtures, are often good value. It is now even possible to obtain seedlings reasonably true to colour.

Removal of the seed heads after flowering improves growth and flowering: an impractical task on the smaller Japanese *Azaleas* but well worthwhile on the larger types. All types can be grown in tubs and troughs, the Japanese being especially suitable for this. Be sure to keep tubs well watered during the summer months with lime-free water, preferably rain water.

Azalea gall is a disease which sometimes causes gardeners concern. Red and pale green swellings, the galls, produce white floury spores. Such galls should be removed and burnt as soon as they are seen. In the unlikely event of a severe attack, use a protective spray of either Bordeaux mixture or Zineb to prevent further spread. Benlate is said to give complete control.

Azalea mollis

Azalea 'Cecile'

Phyllostachys aurea

BAMBOOS

Arundinaria murieliae

While the dense growth and tropical appearance of Bamboos in the garden can be very useful, this group of plants is not as commonly planted as it deserves. We list the whole group here under the name Bamboo because most people refer to the group naming and each nursery tends to offer different forms.

It is perhaps fortunate that we have the name "Bamboo" because some of the latin names are real tongue-twisters. One of the most widely listed is *Arundinaria murieliae,* which reaches 2.5 to 3.5 m in height and can be grown both as a specimen and in tubs. Similar but with purple-black canes and narrower leaves is *Arundinaria nitida,* a very hardy plant.

There is variety of form in leaf and cane colour with *Phyllostachys flexuosa* growing 2.5 to 3 m in height and the canes bright green when young and slightly zig-zagged in shape. This plant forms a dense screen and if an even larger screen is wanted the *Phyllostachys viridi-glaucescens* grows to 6 m high and has yellow branching canes and broad, pointed and shiny leaves.

Most of the Bamboos are easy to grow in all but heavy clay and waterlogged soils, moist and shaded sites are ideal. Cold northerly and easterly winds can brown the foliage. Plants transplanted from the open ground should be moved in September and March/April and pruned back by one half of their growth, new shoots coming from the base.

BERBERIS

Berberis x stenophylla

Berberis is a large and widely varying group of plants, including evergreen
and deciduous species. All are armed with thorns, some more fiercely than others.
They are grown for the beauty of their flowers, foliage and fruits.

BERBERIS

Berberis thunbergii 'Rose Glow'

Tremendous range of colour and variety of form is offered by the genus *Berberis*, known to some by the common name "Barberry". All of them are armed with sharp thorns, a quality which is encouraging their use in public areas, where damage by vandals is a problem. There are well over one hundred species and numerous cultivars in cultivation today. The flowers range in colour from pale yellow to orange.

For practical purposes two main groups exist. Firstly the evergreens, grown mainly for attractive deep green foliage and often for flowers. Secondly the deciduous types, grown for attractive foliage, especially in autumn, and bright berries.

EVERGREENS

A selection of the more popular kinds includes three with attractive flowers. *B. darwinii*, discovered by Charles Darwin in 1835, is a fine garden plant with small, shiny, dark green leaves, masses of deep yellow flowers in April and purple berries in early autumn. *B. x stenophylla*, used extensively for hedging, is impenetrable and attractive with long arching sprays of yellow flowers in April and May. Single plants will grow to 3 m. high and 2–3 m. across.

4. *B. thunbergii* 'Rose Glow'
5. *B. thunbergii* 'Atropurpurea'
6. *B. thunbergii* 'Atropurpurea Nana'
7. *B. x ottawensis* 'Purpurea'

Berberis thunbergii 'Atropurpurea Nana'

Berberis darwinii

B. verruculosa has small glossy green leaves, white on the underside, which turn colour in the autumn. Single, golden yellow flowers are followed by black fruits with a purple "bloom". Compact plants, little more than a metre in height and width, are produced.

The following is a selection of three, grown more for foliage than flowers: *B. candidula* is used in ground cover schemes because it forms dense low mounds only 1 metre high. It has small, glossy dark green leaves. The *B. x hybrido-gagnepainii* group, including 'Chenaultii', are compact shrubs which grow to 1 m. high and spread, with attractive narrow, crinkled leaves. *B. julian* makes a large plant up to 3 m. high and the dense growth forms an effective screen. Its glossy-green, attractively shaped leaves turn red in the autumn.

DECIDUOUS

Deciduous types are dominated by the *B. thunbergii* cultivars. These excellent garden plants grow little more than 1.5 m. in height and breadth. They have flowers of pale yellow, speckled with red, in spring followed by bright red fruits. *B. thunbergii* itself has light

BERBERIS

green leaves which turn brilliant red in the autumn. Some of its cultivars have even more attractive foliage. For example, *B. t. atropurpurea* has dark bronze foliage in spring and summer, which turns to vivid red in the autumn and *B. t.* 'Atropurpurea Nana' is a 'pint sized' edition, growing slowly to 0.5 m. The latter is ideal for low hedges and for the rock garden. Recent introductions which have aroused considerable interest are *B. t.* 'Rose Glow', with purple leaves striped and flecked pink, and *B. t.* 'Aurea', with very bright yellow leaves.

Of all the *B. thunbergii* hybrids, the cross with *B. vulgaris*, our own native barberry, which produced *B. x ottawensis* 'Purpurea' is outstanding. Up to 2 m. high and upright in habit, the arching branches carry oval leaves of the richest deep purple.

Most *Berberis* will produce strong growth in any well cultivated garden soil and the evergreens will tolerate some shade. To avoid losses when transplanting, the purchase of container plants is strongly recommended.

Pruning should be no more than the judicial removal of weak old growth to retain shape and vigour, the deciduous forms in spring and the evergreens after flowering. These delightful plants can be used as hedges, to cover banks, for ground cover and space filling, as well as specimen plants and in mixed shrub borders. Propagation is by seed and cuttings.

The berries in winter

Berberis thunbergii 'Atropurpurea'
Summer growth.

BUDDLEIA

Buddleia davidii 'Royal Red'

Butterflies are attracted to *Buddleia*, as if by magnetism, to the point that
the plant has been called the "Butterfly Bush". For this reason alone *Buddleias*
are worthy of a place in every garden. Their fragrant flowers can provide
colour from May to September, using a selection of species.

Buddleia *(continued)*

Buddleia alternifolia forms either a large shrub or a small tree, 3 metres or so in height and spread. The arching sprays of fragrant, lilac flowers are produced in June. Reginald Farrer, who introduced the plant to Britain, described it as "a gracious, small-leaved weeping willow, when it is not in flower, and a sheer waterfall of soft purple, when it is": an apt description indeed.

Cultivars of *Buddleia davidii* are by far the most widely planted. They never fail to produce an abundance of showy flower spikes from July to September. Popular examples include: *B. d.* 'Black Night', deep purple; *B.d.* 'Charming', lavender pink; *B. d.* 'Empire Blue'; and *B. d.* 'Royal Red'.

Buddleia globosa provides a complete contrast in colour with its globular, tangerine-orange flowers in June. Commonly called the "Orange Ball Tree", it is virtually evergreen, the leaves falling only in severe weather. It grows to 2.5–3 m. in height and spread.

Any good garden soil is suitable for *Buddleias* but a sunny site is preferred. The way self-sown seedlings grow in rubble and old walls indicates their tolerance to lime and their ability to survive in light, well drained soils.

B. alternifolia and *B. globosa* need only be trimmed to shape after flowering but *B. davidii* responds best to hard pruning in March. In the latter case, the previous year's growth is cut back to within 4–6 cm. of the old wood and results in the production of strong growth and large flower spikes.

While the mixed shrub border is the most common home for *Buddleias*, *B. alternifolia* can be trained against walls. All the listed species are useful for providing a quick screen.

Buddleia 'Purple Prince'

Buddleia davidii 'Empire Blue'

Buddleia alternifolia

Buddleia globosa

BUXUS

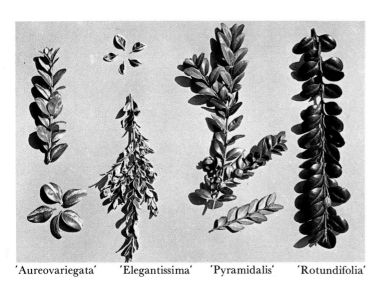

'Aureovariegata' 'Elegantissima' 'Pyramidalis' 'Rotundifolia'

Buxus sempervirens and *Salvia officinalis* 'Tricolor'

Buxus sempervirens is perhaps best known either as an edging to the Victorian vegetable garden or as neatly trimmed topiary specimens. This, the "Common Box", grows to form a large shrub and eventually a small tree up to 10 m. high. It is popular for the masses of luxuriant glossy dark evergreen foliage, which are valuable both on the plant and cut. There are a number of forms in cultivation, many of which are excellent garden plants.

B.s. 'Aureovariegata' forms a shrub up to 3 m. high, of rather loose habit, with leaves striped and mottled golden yellow. B.s. 'Elegantissima' is more compact and slower growing, the leaves being irregularly margined creamy-white.

B.s. 'Pyramidalis' has rich dark green leaves and an erect habit which makes it suitable for hedges. *B.s.* 'Rotundifolia' is a smaller form with neat rounded leaves.

B.s. 'Suffruticosa', the dwarf form, is used as an edging to paths and borders.

All are easy to grow and thrive in both sun and shade. Any ordinary garden soil is suitable, including those which contain chalk. Transplanting of specimens from the open field is best undertaken in September/October and March/April. Pot grown plants can, of course, be planted all the year round.

Any pruning, which includes the trimming of topiary specimens and the cutting of hedges, is best done in August and September. One of the most useful garden evergreens, it is planted to provide screens, hedges, shelter and edging of all kinds. The coloured foliage types are also used as specimens and in mixed borders.

Small white Box Suckers sometimes feed on the young leaves and cause distortion. This pest is controlled by repeated sprays of Malathion.

CALLICARPA

Quite remarkable berries are the feature of *Callicarpa* and the most popular garden species is *Callicarpa bodinieri giraldii*. The lilac flowers produced in July, although insignificant, are followed by dense clusters of lilac to pale purple fruits, like small evenly coloured pearls, from September to Christmas. The dull pale green leaves turn yellow and red, tinged with purple, in autumn. This shrub, which reaches 2 metres in height, is best used in mixed shrubberies and sited where it will receive some protection from hard frost.

Pruning consists of nothing more than removing branches to retain shape and cutting out old wood. This should be carried out in early spring.

Callicarpa bodinieri giraldii

SHRUBS FOR DIFFERENT SOILS

Acid Soils	Acer Azalea Berberis Calluna Camellia	Cotoneaster Erica Hibiscus Hydrangea Indigofera	Kerria Lonicera Rhododendron Tamarix
Alkaline (Chalk) Soils	Aucuba Berberis Buddleia Buxus Ceanothus Colutea Cotoneaster Deutzia Euonymus	Forsythia Fuchsia Hebe Hypericum Laurus Ligustrum Olearia Philadelphus Potentilla	Rhus Sambucus Senecio Symphoricarpos Syringa Vinca Weigela
Clay Soils	Abelia Aralia Aucuba Berberis Chaenomeles Choisya Colutea Cornus Corylus	Cotinus Cotoneaster Deutzia Escallonia Forsythia Hypericum Mahonia Osmanthus Philadelphus	Potentilla Pyracantha Ribes Rosa Senecio Spiraea Symphoricarpos Weigela
Sandy Soils	Berberis Colutea Cotoneaster Elaeagnus	Hibiscus Indigofera Kerria Ligustrum	Lonicera Salix Tamarix

CALLUNA

Unlike some of the *Ericas* which withstand alkaline soil conditions, none of the *Callunas*, grown in gardens under the common name "Heaths and Heathers", will tolerate chalk. Apart from the no chalk requirement, the major difference between the two is leaf form and, as can be seen from the accompanying pictures, the *Callunas* have softer, thicker leaves.

This greater density of foliage makes the coloured foliage forms particularly attractive and because of this they are a fundamental part of any collection of heathers selected for year round appearance. (See page 66 for the year round collection.)

The cultivars grown for the silver, yellow, golden and red foliage mostly have insignificant flowers. Flowering varies according to cultivar from June to November and most eventually reach a height and spread of 30 cm. All garden forms come from *Calluna vulgaris* the common "Heather" or "Ling of Scotland". In the absence of chalk they are easy to grow, thriving in sandy soils and succeeding in quite heavy clays. Poor soils produce compact and more dense growth.

Full sun is required to obtain the best foliage colour and greatest amount of flower. The flower heads should be lightly trimmed back in March every 1–3 years.

A heather border in winter

Calluna vulgaris 'Gold Haze'

Calluna vulgaris 'H.E. Beale'

CAMELLIA

These plants are the hardy shrub equivalent of orchids. The exotic, waxy flowers catch the eye of every would-be gardener and the plant is at last finding its rightful place as a frequently planted subject in smaller gardens. The handsome glossy evergreen foliage is reason enough for planting. The species and cultivars usually listed are quite hardy and under favourable conditions, will grow at least 2 metres high and 1–2 metres across.

A variety of flower forms are offered by most nurserymen, from single, with bright yellow stamens, to semi-double, fully double and anemone flowered types. *Camellia japonica* has hundreds of cultivars and is the most popular species. The following are well established and recommended: *C.j.* 'Adolphe Audusson', semi-double, blood red with contrasting yellow stamens; *C.j.* 'Donckelarii', semi-double pink, often flecked white; *C.j.* 'Elegans' (syn. *C.j.* 'Chandleri Elegans'), deep pink anemone flowered; and *C.j.* 'Mathotiana Rosea', a clear pink double. Less widely offered, but rightly considered to be one of the best for garden planting, is the hybrid *Camellia x williamsii*. The clone, *C. x williamsii* 'J.C. Williams', is single and blush pink. *C. x w.* 'Donation' is larger flowered, pink and semi-double. Very free flowering, these hybrids provide colour from January to May, depending upon the site.

Although the plant is hardy, the flowers, being produced in the winter and early spring, need protection from early morning sun after frost. In more northerly districts a sunny site is required to ripen the wood and encourage the production of flower buds. All *Camellias* dislike lime and chalk. Incorporation of peat and regular mulching, both with peat and leaf mould, is needed where the soil tends to be alkaline. Pruning is best done in April, when thin and straggling shoots can be removed.

These plants are useful as specimens, in mixed borders, as wall plants and, perhaps best of all, in tubs and pots. Regular watering with either lime-free or rain water is needed to avoid flower bud drop.

CARPENTERIA

Fragrant, single, rose-like flowers are a feature of this evergreen. It is best planted with the protection of a wall, a south facing one in cold areas. Two to 3 metres in height and 1.5–2 metres spread, *Carpenteria californica* flowers in June and July.

Any well-cultivated garden soil, lime-free or alkaline, produces strong growth. It can be raised from seed but the seedlings are variable in flower quality and the selected garden cultivars like *C. c.* 'Ladham's Variety' are worth seeking out.

Carpenteria californica

CARYOPTERIS

Caryopteris x clandonensis

The Blue Spiraea, *Caryopteris x clandonensis*, with its greyish-green aromatic leaves, is a useful garden plant. Masses of bright blue flowers are produced on the low arching branches of this shrub from August to October. Growing little more than 1 metre in height and spread, it thrives in virtually every soil type, especially chalk. It is best suited to a well drained site, in full sun.

Caryopteris x clandonensis 'Arthur Simmonds' is an excellent bright blue form and *C. x c.* 'Ferndown' has darker, violet-blue flowers. All cultivars are best pruned hard in February/March when last season's flowered wood should be cut back to 5 cm. from the old wood.

A mixed shrub border is the perfect setting for this plant. Groups should be sited to the front of such borders, where the low-growing habit can be fully seen.

CEANOTHUS

Ceanothus 'Gloire de Versailles'

Ceanothus 'Burkwoodii'

Ceanothus impressus

Amongst blue-flowering garden shrubs, *Ceanothus* is one of the best. All are natives of California, under which climatic conditions almost all are evergreen. Under European conditions the many species are best considered in two groups: those with small but dense and attractive leaves, which in Britain remain evergreen, and the larger leaved types, whose leaves fall in the autumn. A good collection will provide flowers from May to October.

All require a warm site in full sun and a well drained soil. The evergreens need the additional protection of a south or west facing wall. They have fluffy blue flower heads effervescing over arching shoots, which reach a height and spread of 4 metres. Cultivars are best selected according to the time of year flowers are required. *Ceanothus* 'A. T. Johnson' grows vigorously to form a large bush. It flowers in May/June and again in the autumn. *C.* 'Autumnal Blue' is one of the hardier evergreens, flowering from July onwards. *C.* 'Burkwoodii', of medium size, flowers in summer and autumn. *C. dentatus* and *C. impressus* are the two most popular species, flowering May/June.

Deciduous kinds have larger and looser clusters of flowers, which are produced from July to October. Most popular is the sky blue *C.* 'Gloire de Versailles'. Darker in colour and more compact is *C.* 'Topaz'. For a complete change of colour, there is the less common *C.* 'Marie Simon', a pale pink.

Cold, wintry weather may damage the soft young shoots and these are best pruned back to green wood in April. Other than this the evergreen types need little pruning, other than trimming to retain their shape after they have flowered. The deciduous kinds are best pruned by cutting the flowered shoots hard back to within 8 cm. of the previous year's wood in March.

Ceanothus 'Edinburgh'

Ceanothus 'Marie Simon'

CERCIS

Cercis siliquastrum

According to legend, Judas Iscariot hanged himself on *Cercis siliquastrum,* and
as a result this plant carries the common name "Judas Tree". The attractive, pea-shaped
flowers wreathe the branches in May before the distinctive rounded leaves appear.
Its small bushy form makes *Cercis* an adaptable garden tree. Full sun and a
well drained soil are required and the greatest quantity of flower is produced in the
south of the country. It is usually offered in shrub form by British nurserymen and
slowly grows into a rounded tree to 5 metres in height and spread.

CHAENOMELES

see also cover picture
Chaenomeles x superba 'Crimson and Gold'

*Chaenomeles
speciosa* 'Simonii'

Chaenomeles x superba 'Coral Sea'

Chaenomeles x superba 'Pink Lady'

Outstanding garden plants, the *Chaenomeles* are perhaps better known by their previous generic name *Cydonia* than their common names "Japanese Quince" and "Japonica". Being completely hardy and thriving in all soils and sites, they are perhaps the gardener's dream. Attractive spring flowers are followed, in the autumn, by golden yellow fruit, which can be used to make jelly. All this on a small to medium sized shrub, growing up to 4 metres in height and spread.

Chaenomeles speciosa (syn. *Cydonia japonica*), when raised from seed, produces a range of flower colours, predominantly red. Named cultivars are much more worthwhile and a popular selection includes: *C. s.* 'Nivalis', a large pure white; *C. s.* 'Simonii', a semi-double blood red of compact habit; and *C. s.* 'Umbilicata', a deep salmon pink.

The cultivars of *Chaenomeles x superba* are equally, if not more, worthwhile. Beautiful flowers are produced year after year on such well known kinds as: *C. x s.* 'Crimson and Gold', which has bright crimson petals contrasting with golden anthers; *C. x s.* 'Knap Hill Scarlet', orange-scarlet; and *C. x s.* 'Rowallane', which has large, blood-red flowers. There are orange and pink cultivars also, but nothing can beat the brilliant reds for a north wall. When planted and trained against a wall, pruning is best undertaken during the summer after flowering. Next year's flowering spurs are formed by cutting back young shoots to a few centimetres. In practice little pruning is required, especially if sprays of opening buds are cut for indoor decoration.

The presence of thorns encourages the use of this plant in public places where damage by vandals is a problem. It can be used to furnish banks and low walls, planted to the front of mixed shrub borders, grown in deep troughs and trimmed to form a low hedge.

Chaenomeles flower and young fruit.

CHIMONANTHUS

"Winter Sweet" is a perfect common name for this delightful plant, whose flowers bring fragrance through the winter months, from December to February. Its willow-like deciduous leaves and bushy growth, to 3 m. in height and spread, are quite ordinary but its unusual flowering period and powerful scent are adequate reasons for adding this plant to the garden shrub collection.

The species *Chimonanthus praecox* is quite hardy and has cup-shaped flowers 2 cm. across. Less commonly found in catalogues, but worth seeking out, are *C.p.* 'Grandiflorus', which has deeper yellow flowers with red centres and *C.p.* 'Luteus' has larger primrose yellow flowers.

A well drained soil and sheltered site is the ideal. *Chimonanthus* thrives on chalky soils and revels in the protection of a south or west facing wall. It can be planted in a mixed border and as a specimen in lawns and borders.

All the pruning that is necessary will usually be undertaken by cutting sprays for indoor decoration. Any additional pruning is best done in spring. Be patient for the arrival of the first flowers: the plant needs several years to reach maturity and commence flowering, but it is worth waiting.

Chimonanthus praecox.

CHOISYA

Choisya ternata

"Mexican Orange Blossom" is the common and very suitable name for *Choisya ternata*. In May heavenly fragrance from the flowers makes it ideal for patios and beds beneath windows. The shiny, dark green leaves are also aromatic when crushed.

In mild and sheltered gardens it will grow to 2 metres in height and spread. Whilst tolerant of some shade, it is best grown in full sun. In cold areas it requires the protection of a wall to reduce damage by wind and frost. Any well drained garden soil suits it and pruning involves no more than the removal of frost-damaged shoots in March. New shoots are freely produced from the base when plants are cut back.

CLERODENDRON

This vigorous growing shrub is planted for its fragrant flowers in August and September, its bright blue berries in autumn and for its attractive autumn coloured foliage. The leaves give off an unpleasant smell when crushed. It grows to 3 metres or so in height and spread, thriving in any well cultivated garden soil. *Clerodendron trichotomum* will respond to hard cutting in April if it has outgrown its space, but, other than that, pruning is restricted to the removal of any frost-damaged tips in spring.

Clerodendron trichotomum. Fruit with close up of flowers

COLUTEA

Colutea x media

Unusual inflated seed pods are the main feature of *Colutea arborescens*, hence its common name the "Bladder Senna". Yellow pea-shaped flowers are produced, throughout the summer, on loose-growing bushes up to 2 metres in height and spread. The easy-to-grow *Colutea* thrives in hot, dry soil. If its size needs to be limited, really hard pruning can be carried out in March.

CORNUS

'Elegantissima'

'Sibirica'

Cornus mas

Cornus alba 'Sibirica'

Cornus florida 'Rubra'

Coloured foliage and coloured bark are features for which the popular *Cornus*, known to many people as "Dogwoods", are renowned. All of those grown for the colour of their bark succeed in partial shade and in most soils, including chalky, wet and waterlogged conditions.

The best known and most widely planted are cultivars of *Cornus alba*, the "Red-barked Dogwoods", growing to 3 metres high. Two strongly recommended kinds with variegated foliage are *C.a.* 'Elegantissima' and *C.a.* 'Spaethii'. *Cornus stolonifera* is a similar vigorous, suckering shrub, with coloured bark, reaching 3 metres in height. *C. stolonifera* 'Flaviramea' has yellow to lime-green bark and is attractive when planted amongst the red-stemmed kinds.

Two *Cornus* grown for flowers rather than bark and foliage are *Cornus mas*, the "Cornelian Cherry", and *Cornus florida*. *Cornus mas* is grown for the masses of yellow flowers carried on the bare branches throughout February. Several cultivars, not widely listed but worth seeking out, have variegated foliage, for example *C.m.* 'Elegantissima', which has yellow leaves, flushed pink.

Cornus florida is more demanding and will not thrive in chalky soils. Where the right conditions can be provided, the most attractive features are their four-bract flowers in June and their coloured leaves in autumn. The flowers of *C.f. rubra* are rosy pink and the young leaves reddish.

Those of us fortunate enough to have good garden soil on the acid side can also try the uncommon *Cornus kousa chinensis*, a large shrub which produces eye-catching white bracts, red strawberry-like fruits and crimson autumn leaves.

Pruning is best reserved for the kinds with coloured bark, which should be cut back very hard every other March. This ensures plenty of young growth, which has the brightest coloured bark.

Cornus alba and *Cornus mas* provide some of that sought-after winter colour, both in the garden and, when cut and put in water, material for indoor decoration.

Cornus alba 'Elegantissima'

Cornus alba 'Spaethii'

Cornus alba 'Sibirica'

CORYLUS

Corylus avellana 'Contorta'
against a background of snow

Corylus maxima 'Purpurea'

For most people "Hazel" brings to mind the long yellow catkins to be seen in the hedgerows. The native species *Corylus avellana* has several close cousins that are attractive garden plants. They all grow in a wide range of soil types, including chalk, and will survive both full sun and partial shade. The nearest to the wild plant is *Corylus avellana* 'Contorta', which, as is indicated by its common names "Corkscrew Hazel" and "Harry Lauder's Walking Stick", can be quite a conversation piece. Curiously twisted branches grow slowly to reach 3 metres in height. These become a feature when seen dripping with yellow catkins in February.

Quite different, but equally attractive, is the "Purple-leaf Filbert", *Corylus maxima* 'Purpurea'. Its colour is quite as rich as that of the Purple-leaved Beech and has purple catkins in early spring. A contrasting group can be achieved by planting it near the slower growing *Corylus avellana* 'Aurea', a yellow-leaved form.

Pruning can be undertaken in March, after flowering, when old wood, four years of age or more, can be cut back to stimulate the production of strong new branches. Twiggy laterals, the side shoots from main branches, carry the catkins and should be retained. The "Corkscrew Hazel" is used by floral arrangers and for indoor decoration. Cutting for this purpose will usually be more than sufficient pruning.

Cotinus coggygria 'Royal Purple'

COTINUS

Cotinus coggygria in flower

Previously called *Rhus cotinus* and still referred to by the common name "Smoke Tree", *Cotinus coggygria* is grown for its fluffy flower heads and attractive leaves. Rounded bushes up to 3 metres in height and spread are produced in any well-drained garden soil. A profusion of flowers combined with the finest autumn leaf colour occurs on light sandy loams. Rich soils encourage leaves at the expense of flowers and reduce the brightness of autumn colour. The wispy flowers, which give the appearance of smoke from a distance, develop freely in June and July and turn smokey-grey as they age. Smooth, rounded leaves turn from mid-green to bright yellow before they fall in autumn.

Cotinus coggygria 'Royal Purple' has rich purple leaves which turn to various shades of light red in the autumn. This really is a most eye-catching and attractive shrub. *C.c.* 'Notcutt's Variety' is a particularly fine form. The flowers are a mixture of pink and purple.

Pruning is unnecessary but any unwanted growth can be cut out in March. It makes an excellent plant for a mixed border and for use as a lawn specimen. *(see page 17)*

For *Rhus* see page 114

COTONEASTER

Cotoneaster franchetii

These are amongst the most important hardy shrubs both for garden and landscape use. Brilliant berries and autumn foliage colour are their main qualities. There are both evergreen and deciduous kinds and a wide variety of habit and form. It would be fair to say that there is a *Cotoneaster* for every site, soil and function, from lowest ground cover to free standing trees.

FOLIAGE OF COTONEASTER

1. *Cotoneaster salicifolius* 'Parkteppich'
2. *Cotoneaster salicifolius* 'Repens' syn. C. s. 'Avondrood'
3. *Cotoneaster salicifolius*

4. *Cotoneaster* 'Cornubia'
5. *Cotoneaster x watereri*

6. *Cotoneaster lacteus*
7. *Cotoneaster simonsii*
8. *Cotoneaster franchetii* **sternianus**

9. *Cotoneaster horizontalis*
10. *Cotoneaster dammeri*

COTONEASTER

Cotoneaster salicifolius

Cotoneaster x watereri

Cotoneaster glaucophyllus

Ease of culture and attractive form are the most likely reasons for extensive planting of *Cotoneaster*. All carry an abundance of small white and pink tinted flowers in early summer but their main attraction is the conspicuous berries. In an effort to make selection easier, they are placed here in three groups.

Evergreen *Cotoneasters*

The fully evergreen *Cotoneaster conspicuus* grows to form a dense mound of arching branches 2 metres in height and spread, the small mid-green leaves being hidden by the masses of small berries in autumn. Less than half this size is *C.c.* 'Decorus', free berrying and ideal for banks and rock garden use.

Even better for bank carpeting is *Cotoneaster dammeri*, which grows to only a few centimetres high but each plant will spread over 4 square metres. The perfect ground cover plant, it can be planted in full sun and in the shade of trees and taller growing plants. It can truly be described as a replacement for turf that will never require mowing.

Cotoneaster lacteus is the best evergreen of the genus, its deep green leaves contrasting with the 6–7 cm. trusses of flower. The clusters of fruits turn colour late in the year but remain well into the winter. An excellent shrub and one which grows quickly to form an attractive hedge or screen up to 3 m. high.

One of the toughest and hardiest is *Cotoneaster microphyllus*. Tiny evergreen leaves support the large, globular, scarlet fruits, like jewels on a cushion. Excellent for furnishing walls and for covering banks and other sites where attractive appearance and minimum maintenance is the requirement. The dainty *C.m. thymifolius* is a dwarf shrub with even smaller leaves and worth seeking out.

Cotoneaster glaucophyllus is not commonly listed but makes a fine shrub 4 m. high and carries its berries well into the winter.

One of the most popular of all weeping trees and one of the most suitable for small gardens is *Cotoneaster* 'Hybridus Pendulus'. When grown as a standard it creates an eye-catching picture when festooned with brilliant red berries in the autumn. If grown as a low shrub without training, the arching branches form the perfect cover for a bank. This way they grow little more than 0.5 m. high and spread to 4 m.

Cotoneaster salicifolius, which grows 4–5 m. in height and spread, exhibits graceful arching branches bearing clusters of bright berries in the autumn. This variable plant is the parent of several worthwhile garden cultivars. *C.s.* 'Autumn Fire' is a semi-evergreen shrub of weeping habit, with willow-like leaves and masses of scarlet berries. It can be used either for ground cover purposes or trained to produce a small weeping tree. *C.s. flocossus* is similar to the parent in overall size

Cotoneaster 'Hybridus Pendulus'

Cotoneaster lacteus

Cotoneaster microphyllus

COTONEASTER

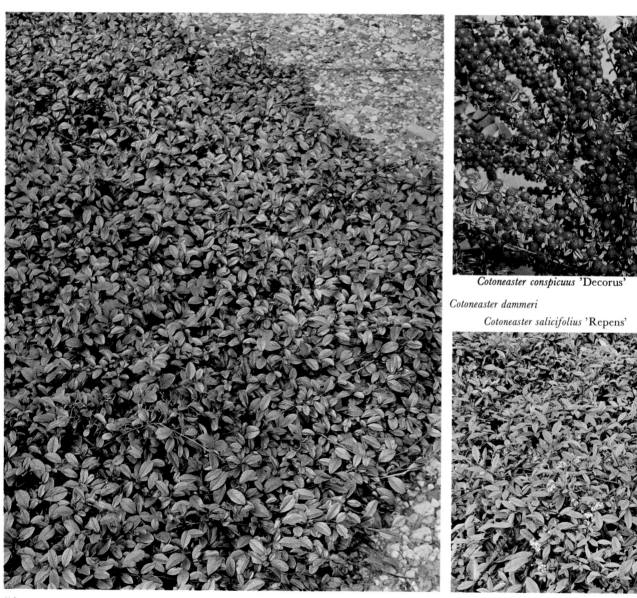

Cotoneaster conspicuus 'Decorus'

Cotoneaster dammeri

Cotoneaster salicifolius 'Repens'

but the leaves are narrower and silky-white on the underside. Gaining rapidly in popularity is *C.s.* 'Parkteppich', another excellent ground covering form, similar to *C.s.* 'Repens' (syn. *C.s.* 'Avondrood'). *Cotoneaster henryanus* is a very similar species.

No list of low-growing, ground-covering *Cotoneasters* is complete without the vigorous *C.* 'Skogholm'. Small oval leaves and bright orange fruits are the features of this plant.

Semi-evergreen *Cotoneasters*

The lines of separation between these groups are not clearly defined and in some seasons, soils and sites the semi-evergreen and deciduous forms hold their leaves for a longer period. *Cotoneaster* 'Cornubia' is one of the strongest, growing 6 m. high. It produces some of the largest fruits of the genus, with heavy bunches weighing down the branches. It can be grown either branching out from soil level, as a shrub or with a clear stem, as a handsome tree.

Cotoneaster franchetii is another graceful shrub, of 2 m. in height and spread, which is grown as much for its attractive form as for its berries and foliage. *C.f. sternianus*, for many years sold under the incorrect name of *C. wardii*, is even more shapely.

Whilst a number of other *Cotoneasters* are used for hedges and screens, *Cotoneaster simonsii* is perhaps the most popular hedge plant. Upright in growth to 2 metres or more, this shrub has leaves which fall to show large scarlet berries held closely to the stem.

Cotoneaster x watereri is of mixed parentage, the result of crosses between *C. frigidus*, *C. henryanus* and *C. salicifolius*. It has a number of named clones, all attractive shrubs growing 4–5 m. high, with red or orange berries. One hybrid from the Watereri group, which must not be forgotten, is the yellow berried *C.* 'Rothschildianus'.

Deciduous *Cotoneasters*

Cotoneaster horizontalis is the best known of all, invaluable for north and east walls, excellent on banks and rich in autumn colour. The common name "Fish Bone Cotoneaster" describes it well. *C.h.* 'Variegatus' is a form with leaves edged white, which is less vigorous than the species.

Of similar form but not growing as flat as *C. horizontalis* is *Cotoneaster adpressus praecox*. The arching branches carry large bright scarlet berries to 1 m. high and 2 m. across.

Cotoneaster divaricatus is my final choice in this selection, a good all-rounder which grows up to 2 m. in height and spread and is reliable for its autumn colour.

For Cotoneasters cultural instructions are simple because almost any position is suitable, including sunny sites and dry soils.

Seedlings vary tremendously and it is much better to plant material propagated from the true species, cultivars and clones. Any trimming, cutting back and pruning is best done in spring.

Cotoneaster adpressus praecox

Cotoneaster x watereri

Cotoneaster horizontalis

Crataegus oxyacantha 'Punicea'

CRATAEGUS

The thorn, well known by the common names "May", "Quickthorn" and "Hawthorn", is less well known by its proper latin name *Crataegus monogyna*. Whilst a number of its cultivars are used in gardens, including *C.m.* 'Biflora', the "Glastonbury Thorn", it is a mixture of this British native and the other, less common, native *Crataegus oxyacantha* which produced the popular flowering thorn trees.

Whilst pink forms of *C. oxyacantha* can be found wild only the single flowered clone *C.o.* 'Punicea' has single scarlet flowers. It is the doubles which are most popular however, with red, pink and white flowers well catered for: *C.o.* 'Plena', white; *C.o.* 'Rosea Flore Pleno', pink; and *C.o.* 'Paul's Scarlet' (syn. *C.o.* 'Coccinea Plena'), scarlet.

All are very hardy and, once established, withstand drought, exposure to cold wind and even some waterlogging. If three and four-year-old trees are slow to break into growth after transplanting, they need to be kept staked and well watered until growth is made. When the type species (Quickthorn) is used for hedging, small plants are set 30–45 cm. apart.

Thorns can be pruned hard to limit their size; July and August is a good time for this. The disease "Fireblight" turns leaves and young shoots black before the branches themselves die back, leaving the black withered leaves hanging. Infected plants should be removed and burned to prevent spread.

Crataegus oxyacantha 'Plena'

Crataegus oxyacantha 'Paul's Scarlet'

An attractive avenue of flowering thorns

CYTISUS

Few plants challenge the hybrid "Brooms" for production of flower

Tumbling sprays of flowers, like water from a waterfall, are a feature of the "Brooms",
both the native *Cytisus scoparius* and the many other species and hybrids, which make
excellent garden plants. All have sweet pea-shaped flowers and many are leafless for the
greater part of the year. The arching green branches, a feature in themselves, are coveted
by flower arrangers who wish to put line and flow into their designs.

CYTISUS

Cytisus x praecox

A group of *Cytisus* hybrids

A selection with the typical broom habit includes: *Cytisus* 'Burkwoodii', cerise and crimson flowers; and *Cytisus* 'Hollandia', cerise and cream flowers, both strong growing hybrids, 2 m. in height and spread, flowering May/June. *Cytisus x praecox* is a near perfect plant for the smaller garden because of its delightful weeping form and abundance of pale cream flowers in April. The flowers have a heavy and unpleasant smell and for this reason are best sited away from the house. The cultivar *C. x p.* 'All Gold', with deeper yellow flowers, and the white *C. x p.* 'Albus' are also recommended for small garden use. Both grow to little more than a metre. Named clones from the native *Cytisus scoparius* are perhaps the most commonly planted. There are many of them and popular examples are *C. s.* 'Andreanus' and *C. s.* 'Goldfinch' with crimson and yellow flowers; *C. s.* 'Golden Sunlight', yellow; and *C. s.* 'Cornish Cream'.

Fast gaining in popularity are the prostrate and low growing types, which are used for low maintenance ground cover.

Cytisus x beanii grows little more than 0.5 m. high and spreads to cover one square metre; *Cytisus x kewensis* spreads even more to provide layers of dense flowers; *Cytisus purgans* is more erect and has stiff branches growing to 1 m. in height and spread. All have cream or yellow flowers in April/May. *Cytisus purpureus* provides colour variation, with purplish flowers in June/July, on plants up to 1.5 m. in height and 1 m. spread.

Most garden soils are acceptable for these plants, although the extremes of acid and chalk are best avoided. All require good drainage and full sun.

Young plants must be container grown to avoid root disturbance and, once established, they do not take kindly to transplanting. Any pruning is best done after flowering by cutting back, by up to two thirds, the previous summer's growth. Once the wood has hardened it does not respond to pruning, hence leggy specimens, especially of *C. scoparius,* are best replaced by young plants.

Brooms have a variety of uses, including beds and borders for hybrids, solitary specimen planting of shapely types like *C. x praecox* and ground cover planting of *C. x kewensis.* Bold splashes of colour can be introduced into mixed borders by siting the taller kinds, which tend to become leggy, towards the back.

Cytisus battandieri, although within this genus, is quite different in form. It grows to become a tall shrub 4 m. or more high, with silky grey-green leaves, similar in shape to *Laburnum.* Upright clusters of bright yellow flowers, which have a sweet fragrance akin to pineapple, are produced in July. It makes a good free-standing specimen plant but thrives best with the protection of a wall.

Cytisus x kewensis

Cytisus scoparius 'Andreanus'

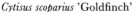

Cytisus scoparius 'Goldfinch'

Cytisus x praecox 'All Gold'

DANAE

Danae racemosa, "Alexandrian Laurel", differs from its close relative the "Butchers Broom" in being bisexual so that every plant may carry bright red berries in autumn and winter. This evergreen is useful both for cutting and for its ability to withstand dense shade and wet soils. It grows to no more than 1 metre high and is of upright growth.

Genista hispanica (See page 74)

DAPHNE

Daphne mezereum

Daphne mezereum

Valuable for its winter flowers and delicious fragrance, *Daphne mezereum* is quite rightly one of the most popular February-flowering garden plants. Stark upright branches, which grow to little more than 1 m. even in the most favourable sites, are clothed with star-like mauve flowers before they break into leaf. The flowers are followed by scarlet berries which are poisonous.

Equally fragrant, but less spectacular in flower, is *Daphne x burkwoodii*, a semi-evergreen which produces clusters of flowers on the tips of shoots in May and June. The good clone *D. x b.* 'Somerset' is the one most commonly listed by nurserymen. More spreading in habit than *D. mezereum*, *D. x burkwoodii* seldom reaches a metre in height.

Well drained soils, including those with some chalk, are suitable but the *Daphnes* must not be allowed to dry out. Both full sun and partial shade are acceptable.

These excellent plants are suitable for the front of shrub borders and around patios and terraces close to the house. When planting near walls, be sure to add plenty of organic matter like peat to the soil to help retain moisture

DEUTZIA

Deutzia x magnifica

DEUTZIA

Deutzia is one of those easy going summer flowering shrubs that are often planted too close in mixed borders and therefore seldom seen at their best. Both single and double flowered forms are available, with flower colour ranging from white through the shades of pink to carmine. There are numerous named clones. The best hybrids include *D.* 'Contraste', large flowers with deep purple band on the back of each petal, *D.* 'Magician', deep pink again with a purple band, and *D.* 'Mont Rose', rose pink.

The several named clones of *Deutzia x magnifica* sold by nurserymen are all free flowering and white in colour. Like the hybrids they grow approximately 2 m. high.

Deutzia x rosea has the delicate characteristics of one of its more tender parents *Deutzia gracilis*, which is one of the best for flowering early under glass. They grow to barely a metre high to form compact plants of truly graceful habit.

Strongest growing of all are the *Deutzia scabra* cultivars. They are erect in habit and grow up to 3.5 m. tall. Nurseries commonly offer *D.s.* 'Plena' (syn. 'Pride of Rochester'), a double white flushed pink.

Virtually any well drained soil will support these plants, although those that are well dug and improved by the addition of peat and compost will induce stronger growth. Open, sunny sites give the most balanced growth but the pink flowered forms hold their colour better given light shade, for example from overhanging trees. Occasional pruning after flowering keeps the plants vigorous and attractive. This is achieved by cutting out old wood from the base. Their natural home is in mixed shrub borders and in screen plantings, but be sure to allow sufficient space for natural development.

Deutzia x Lemoinei

Deutzia 'Mont Rose'

Deutzia x rosea

ELAEAGNUS

E. angustifolia

E. pungens

E. pungens 'Maculata'

Elaeagnus pungens 'Maculata'

Two very useful evergreen plants are to be found under this heading. *Elaeagnus x ebbingei* is a fast growing hybrid, reaching 5 metres high, with leaves that have a white down over the dark green upper surface and a silver scaly reverse. *Elaeagnus pungens* is a tough, occasionally thorned, and somewhat smaller alternative with glossy green leaves. But for colour *Elaeagnus pungens* 'Maculata' should be chosen.

Every leaf has a bold golden splash through the centre, the colour being most pronounced in winter. Both *E. x ebbingei* and *E. p.* 'Maculata' are excellent plants to provide evergreen foliage for cutting, their cut branches being a delight to the floral artist. The taller growing *ebbingei* is better in larger gardens and for screening, while the golden variegated plant has numerous possible uses in the garden, from specimen plant to hedging.

Quite different to the evergreens is *Elaeagnus augustifolia*, a deciduous plant. It grows to 5 metres or more high to form either a loose shrub or a small tree. The branches are thorned and the narrow leaves willow-like and an attractive silver-grey in colour.

None of these are demanding as far as soil and site are concerned, in fact the larger plants provide excellent shelter in exposed and seaside conditions.

Where the evergreens are used for hedging, they are best cut back in June and September.

Any all-green shoots appearing on *E. p.* 'Maculata' and similar variegated forms should be cut out as soon as they are seen.

ERICA

The Silver Birch bark is especially attractive surrounded by *Ericas*

These plants are rapidly increasing in popularity because they are quick to establish, cover the ground rapidly and give year-round flowers if the correct range of species is selected. "Heathers" and "Heaths" are best considered as a group and for general garden purposes this means adding *Calluna* (see page 37) to the genera *Erica*. They are mostly low-growing subshrubs which form rounded mounds up to 0.5 m. in height.

Where the soil contains chalk and is alkaline, the choice rests with predominantly winter flowering *Erica carnea*, *E. mediterranea* and *E. x darleyensis*. The introduction of acid soil to make raised beds or, alternatively the very liberal use of acid peat, allows a wider choice of attractive flowers and foliage to be made. A selection to provide year-round foliage colour will be achieved with the following popular plants: *Calluna vulgaris* 'Golden

Feather'; *C.v.* 'Gold Haze; and *C.v.* 'Silver Queen'. Some *Erica carnea* cultivars will flower from November to March, *Erica x darleyensis* from November to April, *Erica mediterranea* from March to May, *Erica cinerea* from June to August, *E. vagans* from July to October, and *Calluna vulgaris* cultivars such as *C.v.* 'County Wicklow' and *C.v.* 'Peter Sparkes' from August to November.

Healthy young plants spaced 40 cm. or more apart grow very quickly and in two seasons will cover the ground. Mulching annually with very well moistened peat improves their speed of growth and development. The only attention required is the removal of dead flower heads with shears in spring. Do not cut the plants back hard because this spoils their natural shape.

Sudden death, especially during hot weather, can be due to the disease Phytophthera. Affected plants should be burned and the soil surrounding them replaced.

Erica carnea 'Winter Beauty' (syn. 'King George')
and *E. c.* 'Springwood White'

ESCALLONIA

Almost evergreen, the foliage of *Escallonia* is a good foil to the clusters of flowers, which are produced throughout the summer and early autumn and range in colour from pale pink to crimson. There are a number of excellent garden hybrids, including those raised in Northern Ireland which carry the name Donard. Fine and popular examples are *E.* 'Apple Blossom', pink and white flowers, small in habit; *E.* 'C. F. Ball', crimson flowers and vigorous; *E.* 'Donard Seedling', pink buds open white; *E.* 'Edinensis', carmine buds open shell pink. *E. macrantha* is particularly strong and robust and especially suited to hedging.

Most of the *Escallonias* grow to 2.5 m. in height and thrive in widely varying conditions. Any well drained garden soil is suitable and they will survive even in those that are very light and dry. In cold northern areas, except near the coast, they are not completely hardy and the protection of a wall may be needed.

Where they are used for screening and as hedges, sufficient space should be allowed between plants to make hard cutting back unnecessary. Any trimming should be done after flowering.

Escallonia hybrid

Escallonia macrantha

EUONYMUS

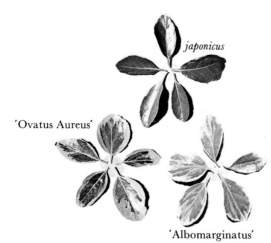

japonicus

'Ovatus Aureus'

'Albomarginatus'

Euonymus japonicus 'Ovatus Aureus'

The wild "Spindle", *Euonymus europaeus,* is well known for its green wood, brilliant autumn leaf colour and rose-red seed capsules enclosing orange seeds. Even brighter is the selected garden plant *Euonymus europaeus* 'Red Cascade', which produces branches 2 metres high, thickly clustered with the rosy red fruits. Whilst this is a valuable plant for the larger garden, there are a number of evergreen *Euonymus* which are gaining more rapidly in popularity because of their compact growth and attractive foliage.

Euonymus fortunei radicans has what is botanically described as juvenile growth and, in effect, will not flower and fruit unless, with age, the quite different adult foliage is produced. It has produced several very attractive sports (freak but permanent changes in growth) such as *E.f. radicans* 'Variegatus' (syn. *E.f. radicans* 'Gracilis') which has greyish-green leaves with white variegation and, at certain times of the year, pink tips to the young shoots. It is an excellent ground cover plant and looks well in association with heathers. *E.f.* 'Carrierei' is the adult form of *E.f. radicans* and it has sported to produce the cultivar *E.f.* 'Silver Queen'. One of the most colourful of all, 'Silver Queen' will grow to 3 m. in height when provided with the protection and support of a wall. The margins of the young leaves are normally creamy-yellow but turn creamy-white as they mature. Two further cultivars rapidly growing in popularity for ground cover use are *E.f.* 'Coloratus' whose leaves turn purple in winter, and *E.f. radicans* 'Vegetus' which flowers and fruits freely.

Brightest of all are the more upright, evergreen, *Euonymus japonicus* cultivars and, although quite hardy, some have sufficient colour for use as indoor foliage plants. *E.j.* 'Albo-marginatus' has green leaves, margined white, and *E.j.* 'Ovatus Aureus' (syn. *E.j.* 'Aureovariegatus) has yellow variegation. Whilst both *Euonymus fortunei* and *Euonymus japonicus* grow well in sun and shade, the variegated forms need full sun to produce the brightest colour.

Attractive hedges can be grown of *Euonymus japonicus* if clipped in April and trimmed again lightly in August.

Euonymus europaeus 'Red Cascade'

Euonymus fortunei radicans 'Variegatus'

EXOCHORDA

Exochorda racemosa

Very attractive in spring, *Exochorda racemosa* forms a shrub of loose, open habit some 4 m. high. Clusters of white flowers, rather like large apple blossoms, smother the branches in May. Chalky soils are not suitable and produce pale, chlorotic leaves. This plant is equally attractive used either as a specimen or in a mixed border.

Euonymus alatus

FAGUS

A hedge of seed raised *Fagus sylvatica purpurea* with plants of varying shades and inset the vegetatively propagated *F. s.* 'Riversii'

Our "Common Beech", *Fagus sylvatica*, makes one of the finest hedges. If trimmed each year the dry brown leaves remain on the plants through the winter to provide screening for virtually twelve months. *F. sylvatica* breaks into growth in a multitude of shades to provide verdant foliage through the summer and rich golden shades in the autumn. There are several purple leaved forms, including the seed raised *F. s. purpurea* and the grafted clone *F. s.* 'Riversii'.

All the *F. sylvatica* cultivars and varieties thrive in chalk and a wide variety of soils, excepting those which are poorly drained and heavy clays. Small plants for hedging should be spaced 30 cm. apart.

FORSYTHIA

Forsythia ovata 'Tetragold'

Forsythia x intermedia 'Spectabilis'

Forsythia x intermedia 'Lynwood'

This is one of the most brilliantly coloured of early spring-flowering shrubs. It is widely planted and popular because of its free flowering nature and ease of culture. The common name "Golden Bell Flower" is less well known than the true generic name. Rich yellow flowers smother the branches in late March and early April, before the leaves, which are mid to dark green, ovate and marginally toothed. This hardy shrub grows with an open habit to 2–3 m. in height and width.

Forsythia x intermedia 'Spectabilis' is the most popular and widely planted cultivar but there are several other excellent hybrids, including 'Lynwood' and 'Arnold Giant'.

The latter is smaller than the first two, growing to 1 m. high and to 2 m. across.

'Beatrix Farrand' is a larger plant, resulting from a cross between 'Arnold Giant' and *F. ovata*, and has large flowers over 2.5 cm. across.

(Continued overleaf)

Forsythia used for hedging.

Forsythia x intermedia 'Spectabilis'

FORSYTHIA
(continued)

Forsythia ovata is early flowering and compact, growing to 1.5 m. high, and *F. o.* 'Tetragold', a cultivar of recent introduction, is also excellent for the small garden.

Forsythia suspensa has a rambling, weeping form and is effective trained against walls, even those with a northerly aspect. It can also be used on steep banks and sprawling over walls and fences. It thrives in exposed sites and tolerates city conditions. Good specimens can be seen in widely varying soil types and any reasonable garden soil will give satisfactory growth.

Pruning of all types need be nothing more than the removal of old flowering shoots immediately after flowering. Excessively hard pruning will encourage lush growth at the expense of flowers. Sometimes natural layers will occur where low branches come into contact with the soil and form roots.

Forsythia is an excellent plant for a mixed shrubbery, for screening and for use as a hedge. Branches cut after Christmas can be taken indoors and placed in water to be forced into flower for indoor decoration. A few strands of black cotton, through the branches, will stop birds damaging the flower buds.

FUCHSIA

Fuchsia 'Riccartonii'

Hardy fuchsias, although cut back by frost, survive most winters and produce new shoots from the base in spring.

They bear an abundance of pendant flowers 3–5 cm. long on slender arching branches throughout the summer. In sheltered sites and coastal areas, where the wood is not damaged by frost, they grow 1.5 to 2 m. high but where growth is renewed each year, only reach 1 m. in size.

The most commonly planted is *Fuchsia* 'Riccartonii', a popular garden plant often used as a hedge or low screen in coastal districts. Slender scarlet sepals with violet centres and long slender flowers are the special qualities of *Fuchsia magellanica*. There is a variegated form, *F. m.* 'Variegata', which has greyishgreen leaves flushed pink and margined cream, and a white flowered form, *F. m.* 'Alba'.

Smaller in stature but very free flowering are *Fuchsia* 'Mrs. Popple', which grows 1 m. high and produces large flowers of scarlet and violet, and *Fuchsia* 'Tom Thumb', 30 cm. in height and carmine and violet flowers.

Both open sunny sites and shade are suitable. Fuchsias grow freely in all garden soils, but those which are moisture retentive and free draining give the best results. Established plants should be pruned back to ground level in spring, except in areas where frost does not cause die-back, when the removal of dead wood is all that is required.

Protection from severe frost can be given by covering the base of the plant with 20–30 cm. of dry peat in the autumn.

SHRUBS WITH FRAGRANT FLOWERS		SHRUBS WITH ATTRACTIVE FRUIT		SHRUBS WITH COLOURFUL AUTUMN FOLIAGE	
Abelia	Osmanthus	Aucuba	Malus	Acer	Hydrangea
Azalea	Philadelphus	Berberis	Pyracantha	Amelanchier	Rhus
Buddleia	Ribes	Callicarpa	Rosa	Azalea	Ribes
Ceanothus	Rosa	Chaenomeles	Sambucus	Berberis	Spiraea
Chimonanthus	Skimmia	Colutea	Skimmia	Callicarpa	Viburnum
Choisya	Syringa	Cotoneaster	Symphoricarpos	Cornus	
Clerodendrum	Viburnum	Daphne	Viburnum	Cotinus	*Climbers*
Daphne		Euonymus		Hamamelis	Parthenocissus
Hamamelis	*Climbers*	Hippophae	*Climbers*		
Lonicera	Jasminum	Hypericum	Lonicera		
Magnolia	Wisteria	Ilex	Passiflora		
Mahonia		Leycesteria	Clematis		
		Mahonia			

GARRYA

Garrya elliptica,
close up of catkins.

Garrya elliptica

The glossy evergreen foliage of *Garrya elliptica* is as good as laurel but deeper in colour and equally able to withstand the onslaught of city smoke and dirt. If the foliage is not reason enough for including this plant in any collection, as a bonus the male plants produce long slender silver-green catkins in January and February, which turn pale yellow as pollen is released.

In northerly areas cold winds "burn" the softer growth and in such conditions some protection may be needed. Ideally a south-facing wall provides this but in milder areas *Garrya* will survive on those difficult sites facing north. Sited against a wall *Garrya* grows 5 m. high and to a similar width.

The dark evergreen foliage is valuable in mixed shrub collections and the catkins are a feature of both free standing and wall specimens in winter. They grow easily in ordinary, well cultivated garden soils.

Pot and container grown plants are advised if transplanting losses are to be avoided. Pruning is likely to be done when collecting pieces for indoor decoration. Any other trimming back should be done after flowering, in early spring.

GENISTA

Genista lydia

Closely related to *Cytisus* and having, for several species, the same common name "Broom", *Genista* provides a number of low-growing, floriferous garden plants. Two are particularly useful. *Genista hispanica*, with the common name "Spanish Gorse", produces a semiglobular shrub 1 metre in radius. Its densely spined, gorse-like growth is smothered by bright yellow pea-shaped flowers in June. *Genista lydia* has much more typical broom-like growth. Slender grey-green branches of semi-prostrate habit reach up to 1 m. in height and spread to 2 m. Clusters of flowers festoon the branches in May and June. Both are excellent plants for covering dry banks and *G. hispanica* is excellent in large plant troughs. They revel in hot, sunny sites and whilst all well drained soils support their growth, poor soils produce the most flower.

(See pages 10 and 60)

HAMAMELIS

The sweet smelling "Witch Hazel" is quite rightly one of the most popular garden shrubs. Good specimens in flower bring as much interest and colour to the garden in mid-winter as does *Forsythia* in spring. The almost circular, midgreen leaves can easily be mistaken for the wild hazel and in autumn they turn bright yellow. While *Hamamelis mollis* is probably the best known and most widely planted, *H. m.* 'Pallida' is worth seeking out. Bold sulphur-yellow flowers are carried in abundance on the naked branches. Small branches can be cut to bring the strong sweet scent into the house.

A good garden soil heavily enriched with peat or leaf mould to retain moisture encourages strong growth. They are not easy plants to propagate, the named cultivars being grafted, and for this reason stocks are often limited. Plants are best sited with a dark background in winter to contrast with the yellow flowers.

Hamamelis mollis

HEBE

Hebe

The neat and compact forms of *Hebe* are very useful garden plants for ground cover. Most species originated from New Zealand. Previously listed under the genus *Veronica* and still referred to as such, as its common name, their main quality is shiny evergreen leaves. *Hebe brachysiphon* (syn. *H. traversii*), which has small mouse-ear-like leaves and white flower spikes in June and July, and *Hebe* 'Autumn Glory', with larger leaves and purple flower spikes from June to the frost, are popular examples. They grow to little more than 0.5 m. high and form a rounded bush. Quite a different leaf form is provided by *Hebe armstrongii* with golden-green string-like foliage.

A number of low growing forms are being used increasingly in planting schemes designed for minimum maintenance. *H.* 'Carl Teschner', with dark green leaves and purple flowers, and *H. pinguifolia* 'Pagei', with silver-grey leaves and tiny white flowers, are two excellent examples.

Well drained soil is best but *Hebe* grow well in most gardens. They withstand the dust and grime of cities and are excellent coastal plants. Most are damaged by the prolonged severe cold which can occur in northern districts.

HIBISCUS

Hibiscus syriacus 'Woodbridge'
Hibiscus syriacus 'Blue Bird'

"The nurserymens' nightmare" could well be the common name for this, one of the most free flowering shrubs of late summer. It is one of the last plants to break into growth in spring and many a newcomer to gardening, impatient to see a recently transplanted specimen show signs of new leaf, will return it to his supplier in despair. However, there is no need for concern; the late start into growth is fully compensated by the hollyhock-like flowers when they burst into bloom.

There are a number of colourful single and double cultivars, including the five illustrated here.

H. s. 'Blue Bird' has flowers quite 8 cm. across. Most gardens contain suitable sites but deep, well drained, easily worked soil is the ideal. Protection will be required throughout the winter for plants in cold northern areas. Growth is upright and in favourable, warm and sunny sites will reach 2 m. high. Pruning should aim at keeping the plants vigorous. Early spring pruning, combined with feeding, will encourage flowers, which occur on young shoots of the current year's growth.

Single plants, given plenty of space to develop, grow to a plump, neatly rounded shape. They are quite spectacular in flower and can be used as solitary plants as well as in mixed shrub borders.

Hibiscus syriacus 'Roseus Plenus'

Hibiscus syriacus 'Lady Stanley'

HIPPOPHAE

Hippophae rhamnoides

"Sea Buckthorn" is the well known common name for *Hippophae rhamnoides*, a strong growing shrub up to 5 m. high. Well suited to exposed and windy conditions, it is a common plant for coastal planting. Silver-grey leaves fall in the autumn to expose an abundance of bright orange berries. The rather coarse growth and fierce thorns of *Hippophae* demand a garden of some size unless it can be planted to form a protective shelter belt.

Most garden soils are suitable and this shrub is adapted especially to dry, sandy conditions. Male and female plants and wind to blow the pollen are needed to provide the annual crop of berries. Little pruning is needed and hedges are best trimmed in August.

Hibiscus syriacus 'Duc de Brabant'

HYDRANGEA

The range of colour and form of the "Hortensias",
a group of *Hydrangea macrophylla* hybrids,
can be seen from these illustrations.

Hydrangea paniculata 'Grandiflora'

Hydrangea macrophylla 'Lacecap'

While the greater number of *Hydrangea macrophylla* cultivars are raised to be forced as early flowering pot plants, they remain a very popular garden plant and many of the forced specimens are planted outside, when they have finished flowering. Suburban front gardens abound with them and, given warmth and moisture, they produce annually masses of bold flower heads. There are white flowering cultivars, *H. m.* 'Madame E. Mouilliere' is a good one, as well as pink, red and blue. The blue varieties will turn pink or mauve in alkaline soils. As long as the soil is not very alkaline an application of blueing powder every 14 days throughout the growing season will ensure a good blue flower colour.

Another *H. macrophylla* group is the "Lacecaps". The flower heads are flat, with an outer ring of large florets and many tiny florets in the centre, which gives the appearance of old lace. They require treatment similar to the Hortensias.

Much hardier is *Hydrangea paniculata* 'Grandiflora', which produces large cone-shaped white flower heads to terminate the current season's growth. Larger flowers are produced by pruning all one-year old wood hard in the early spring.

All *Hydrangeas* are greedy feeders so that rich soils, with plenty of moisture-retaining material like peat and compost incorporated, are needed for vigorous growth. The *H. macrophylla* cultivars are not completely hardy and protection from severe frost is advisable, using straw or sacking. With the exception of *H. paniculata*, little pruning is needed apart from the removal of dead flower heads in March. The fading flowers are quite attractive and provide some winter protection, so removal before March is not recommended.

Apart from their use grouped together in garden borders, the Hortensias are excellent for patio decoration and for planting in tubs and troughs. Plants in tubs need regular watering in the summer, preferably with rain water.

HYPERICUM

Hypericum 'Hidcote'

Hypericum 'Hidcote' **close up of flowers.**

Yellow buttercup-like flowers are produced by all species and cultivars of *Hypericum*. The low growing *Hypericum calycinum*, "Rose of Sharon", is used extensively as evergreen ground cover but the taller, semi-evergreen shrubs are more suited to the average garden. One of the most popular is *Hypericum* 'Hidcote'. Quite hardy, this grows no more than 2 metres in size and produces masses of large golden yellow flowers from July to October. Smaller in growth and flower size is *Hypericum x inodorum* 'Elstead', it carries bright salmon red berries and purplish leaf tints in the autumn to compensate for the smaller flowers.

Less hardy and much less invasive than *H. calycinum* is *H. x moserianum* 'Tricolor'.

The bright yellow flowers are almost an unnecessary embellishment to the brightly variegated white and green leaves, that are also tinged pink. *H. x moserianum* itself has green leaves, grows 0.5 metres high and is a good dwarf shrub for ground cover use and where summer colour is required.

Very accommodating plants, forms of *Hypericum* can be planted in full sun and semi-shade. They will withstand dry soil conditions and grow freely in virtually all but waterlogged gardens. Once established *H. calycinum* is particularly tough and more than holds its own against weeds in the competition for light and moisture under trees and in impoverished sites. Rust disease can be a problem with *H. x i.* 'Elstead'.

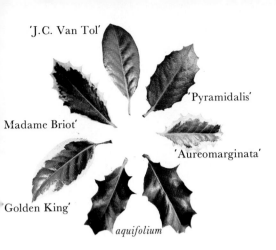

'J.C. Van Tol'

'Pyramidalis'

Madame Briot'

'Aureomarginata'

'Golden King'

aquifolium

ILEX

Ilex aquifolium

The evergreen "Common Holly", *Ilex aquifolium,* is as useful in the garden all the year round as it is popular for its seasonal bright berries at Christmas. This interesting subject has male and female flowers on separate plants, a fact confusingly illustrated by *Ilex aquifolium* 'Silver Queen', a male form with white-margined leaves, and the female *Ilex x altaclarensis* 'Golden King', an excellent golden variegated form. Needless to say the king and queen need planting together for pollination but it is the king that produces the berries! In other words male plants must pollinate the females for the production of berries.

Two widely planted self-fertile cultivars are the almost spineless *Ilex x altaclarensis* 'J. C. van Tol', which produces regular heavy crops of berries, and *Ilex aquifolium* 'Pyramidalis', another prolific fruiting form with leaves more heavily thorned near the base of the plant. *Ilex a.* 'Pyramidalis Fructuluteo' is one of the yellow-berried forms.

From the many garden forms of holly the following is a popular selection. Colourful variegation is well illustrated by the female *Ilex aquifolium* 'Madame Briot' whose leaves are margined and blotched deep yellow, and *Ilex a.* 'Aureomarginata', a name which refers to a group of clones with yellow margined leaves. The "Hedgehog Holly", *Ilex aquifolium* 'Ferox' (male) has somewhat smaller leaves that bear small sharp thorns on the leaf surface as well as on the edges. 'Ferox Argentea' and 'Ferox Aurea' are white and golden-variegated cultivars.

Ilex aquifolium
'Watereriana'

ILEX
(continued)

Ilex cornuta
'Rotunda'

Left untrimmed, most hollies make tall, bushy shrubs and small trees but some forms like 'Ferox' are slower growing and more dwarf. They grow well in all garden soils, preferring slight acidity, which can be obtained by a good application of peat when preparing the site prior to planting. Sites in sun and shade are equally suitable. Like most evergreens, young plants only move satisfactorily when a good ball of soil is retained around the roots. Given this, transplanting can be done at any time through autumn, winter and early spring but the coldest part of the winter is best avoided. If leaves are shed following the shock of transplanting, do not despair, new growth will soon be made. Container grown plants will not suffer a transplanting check.

The hollies make excellent hedge plants, although fallen leaves can play havoc with fingers weeding adjacent borders. Hedges are best trimmed in spring and all plants can be cut hard back because new growth will soon be made, even from the old wood if it receives sufficient light. Specimen plants and those in mixed borders may be pruned to shape in July.

INDIGOFERA

Indigofera gerardiana

Foliage rather like mimosa is the feature of this shrub. Although one of the last plants to break into leaf in spring its open, sprawling habit is most elegant. Growing little more than 1.5 metres in height and spread, the rose-purple, pea-shaped flowers are borne terminally on the arching branches from July to October.

Not completely hardy, *Indigofera gerardiana* is best given the protection of a south facing wall in cold districts. Plants thrive best in sunny situations and in soils that are free draining and on the light, sandy side. Hard frost will damage all growth above ground but strong new replacement shoots will come from the base. Rejuvenation of old woody plants can be brought about by hard pruning in April but little other pruning is necessary.

JASMINUM

"Winter Jasmine", *Jasminum nudiflorum*, is probably the most widely planted true winter-flowering shrub.

The bright yellow flowers on rich green branches are a delight to see from November to March. Easy to grow, with pendant branches which soon take root, they are happy in a very wide range of soil types. Wall protection encourages taller growth but east facing sites should be avoided because swift thawing by the sun, after frost, turns the flowers brown.

The pruning of side shoots after flowering results in new strong lateral growth which flowers freely during the following winter. This is an excellent plant for walls and to cover banks.

Jasminum nudiflorum

KALMIA

Kalmia latifolia

Like *Rhododendron* in its requirement, *Kalmia latifolia* is one of those evergreens for which it is well worth making special soil preparations.

Lime and chalk-free conditions are essential and moist, acidic, peaty soils in semi-shade under trees are the ideal.

Given these cultural requirements, in June clusters of rich pink, five-sided flowers are the reward. Described by some gardeners as pink sugar icing, the flowers are carried against a foil of glossy evergreen leaves. Once established, *Kalmia* grows to 2 metres and the only other attention required is the removal of dead flower heads.

KERRIA

Kerria japonica 'Pleniflora'

The only fault with *Kerria japonica* is its undemanding nature and free-flowering habit. Suckers spring from the base of each plant to form a many-stemmed shrub.

These stems are bright green and quite attractive in their own right after leaf fall.

The species has single yellow flowers, akin to buttercups, in April/May and is more delicately graceful than its showy cultivars.

The double flowered, brassy yellow *Kerria japonica* 'Pleniflora' is the best garden plant.

It grows a little more strongly than the species and reaches 3 metres in height. The creamy-white variegated leaf form, *K.j.* 'Variegata', is dwarf at 1.5 m. and requires the protection of a wall in cold districts.

Almost every soil and site, including shade, is acceptable. Pruning back the flowered shoots in early June encourages strong new growth and plenty of flowers the next year.

KOLKWITZIA

Kolkwitzia amabilis

Another easy-to-grow shrub, *Kolkwitzia amabilis* is not demanding as far as soil and situation are concerned. Its most attractive feature is foxglove-like flowers. The clusters of pink buds open in May and June to show the bell-shaped blooms with their attractive cream throat markings.

The leaves fall in autumn to unmask graceful, arching branches that reach 2–3 metres in height and spread. Because it is at its most attractive in flower, *Kolkwitzia* is best used in borders of mixed shrubs selected perhaps to give year-round effect. Two improved clones worth searching out are *K.a.* 'Rosea' and *K.a.* 'Pink Cloud'.

Any pruning necessary to retain size and shape should be carried out after flowering.

LABURNOCYTISUS

A really "crazy, mixed up" plant is *Laburnocytisus adamii*. Described in technical terms as either a chimera or a graft hybrid, it is a freak combination of the "Common Laburnum" and "Purple Broom", *Cytisus purpureus*. This plant, whose centre is *Laburnum* and bark *Cytisus*, is like a sandwich in which the filling bursts through now and again. Some branches carry the bloom of either one or the other of the original plants, while the remainder produce flowers that are a mixture of the two. Growth and treatment is similar to *Laburnum*.

We have this 'freak-out' purely by chance. It was the result of an accident on a French nursery in the early 1800's and the nurseryman is now immortalised in the name of the plant. At the time *Cytisus purpureus* was being grafted on to *Laburnum*. The scion of *Cytisus* was knocked off leaving the smallest piece behind. Both *Laburnum* stock and the small piece of broom grew to form *Laburnocytisus*. The graft hybrid has been perpetuated by grafting on to *Laburnum*.

Laburnocytisus adamii

LABURNUM

Laburnum x watereri

One of the most popular of all small trees, the *Laburnum*, "Golden Rain Tree", and more especially *Laburnum anagyroides* (syn. L. vulgare), the "Common Laburnum", is ideally suited to the smaller garden. The major disadvantage remains that all parts of this plant are poisonous, the worst being the shiny black seeds. For this reason, *L. x watereri* 'Vossii' is strongly recommended because it sets few seeds and produces masses of great long trusses of yellow flowers.

The blaze of yellow is a real spectacle in May and June with the small trees and tall shrubs, some 6–10 metres and more high, dripping with flowers. The mid-green leaves fall in autumn to expose the shiny green wood. Nearly all garden soils are suitable for this undemanding plant and when it outgrows its space, hard pruning will be repayed by the production of vigorous new growth.

LAURUS

"Sweet Bay" and "Bay Laurel" are names commonly used to describe this attractive evergreen, which is perhaps better known to cooks than gardeners. The illustrated plant is sited a few steps from a kitchen door and many are the journeys made by the lady of the house to secure leaves for flavouring. The flowers are small, inconspicuous, yellowish-green and produced in April.

Most well cultivated soil is suitable and in sheltered sites *Laurus nobilis* grows 4–6 metres high. Severe frost will damage the leaves and young shoots. This plant responds well to pruning and specimens grown in tubs are best pruned twice during the summer to retain the desired shape.

Planted as a specimen and allowed to develop naturally, this plant takes on an attractive pyramidial shape. Sooty, sticky mould on the leaves is caused by scale insects, which occur in the main on tub grown plants, especially those kept under glass. They can be controlled by spraying with Malathion.

Laurus nobilis

LAVANDULA

Lavandula spica 'Hidcote'

The "Old English Lavender", *Lavandula spica*, should be found space in every garden. Few plants have so many qualities and none can rival its fragrance. It is at its best when young and growing strongly to provide well furnished bushy plants fully covered by the attractive silver grey foliage.

There are a number of clones that are better than the species and one of the best is *L.s.* 'Hidcote' with compact growth eventually reaching 0.75 m. in height and spread and deep violet flower spikes. Similar but with leaves greener in colour is *L.s.* 'Munstead'. One of the best for use as a low hedge is *L.s.* 'Vera', commonly called "Dutch Lavender" and growing 1 m. and more in height, with lavender blue flowers.

These plants are not demanding in their soil requirements and the best results are obtained in full sun and well drained soils. The plants should be trimmed back with shears after flowering.

LESPEDEZA

This forms an open plant which is useful where autumn flowering is required. Weeping branches 1.5 metres long carry trusses of rosy-purple, pea-shaped flowers from September to the frost. The three-part leaves are attractive in their own right but appear rather late in the spring. *Lespedeza thunbergii* is best in full sun and in medium to light soils. It is best used as a specimen surrounded by grass.

Lespedeza thunbergii

LEYCESTERIA

Leycesteria formosa

Strong growing and easy to cultivate, *Leycesteria formosa* is used as much as a novelty as an attractive garden plant. It reaches 2 metres in height and each bright green hollow stem carries a long, tassel-like inflorescence in July and August. The white flowers contrast with the dark claret bracts and are followed by purple-black fruits, the traditional reason for including this plant in selections for pheasant covets.

Any reasonably fertile soil is suitable, as is any site—seaside, shade or full sun—but more flowers are produced on plants in full sun. Hard frost may damage the upper branches but these will soon be renewed from the base in spring. Any pruning should be carried out in March.

LIGUSTRUM

Ligustrum ovalifolium   *L.o.* 'Aureum'

Ligustrum ovalifolium 'Aureum'

One of the most widely planted of all shrubs, especially for hedges, is the "Common Privet". It grows some 3–4 metres in height and spread if left unattended but is particularly responsive to clipping and topiary work. The requirement for frequent clipping is now considered a disadvantage by most of us, who seek hedge plants which require only one or two cuts per year.

The white flowers, produced in June, have a rather insipid, if not unpleasant, scent and are of little interest.

All species are virtually evergreen, the leaves falling either in spring as new growth begins or occasionally after a spell of severe winter weather.

By far the most widely planted is *Ligustrum ovalifolium*, the ordinary green-leaved privet. Much more attractive are *L.o.* 'Argenteum', leaves margined creamy-white and *L.o.* 'Aureum', the "Golden Privet", rich yellow leaves with green centres, both of which deserve wider use as less vigorous hedges and as single plants in mixed borders. *Ligustrum japonicum* and its slower growing cultivar *L.j.* 'Rotundifolium' have broad, handsome evergreen foliage and are excellent screening plants.

The native *Ligustrum vulgare* is especially prolific in the production of the black fruits typical of this genus.

L. japonicum   L.o. 'Argenteum'

Ligustrum vulgare

Ligustrum vulgare 'Aureum'

Ligustrum japonicum

Ligustrum ovalifolium

There are various forms such as *L.v.* 'Aureum' with dull yellow leaves.

These adaptable plants grow in a variety of soils and almost any position, even dense shade. The "Golden Privet" is especially recommended for hedges, for use as a specimen, for mixed borders and for floral arrangement work.

LONICERA

This group of plants is best known for the many sweetly scented climbing "Honeysuckles", described in the climbing plant section of this book.

There are, however, a number of shrubby honeysuckles which are valuable garden plants. One, *Lonicera nitida,* is clothed with small evergreen leaves and is often used to form low or medium-sized hedges. These need clipping several times a year to retain their shape and, if more than 1 m. high, they require the support of stakes and horizontal wires to remain upright. Alternatively a mixture of *L. nitida* and seedling beech is attractive and the beech provides the support. *L. nitida* 'Fertilis' (syn. *L. pileata yunnanensis*) is more upright and more vigorous in growth. *L. n.* 'Baggessen's Gold' is a golden-leaved form, which needs full sun for the brightest colour.

Somewhat similar but with larger, 'box' – like leaves and a low spreading habit is *L. pileata.* It is used increasingly as a ground cover plant in the shade of trees, on banks and in beds and borders. The young spring growth is lighter in colour than the mature foliage, forming an attractive contrast. If left unclipped it produces shiny dark violet berries in the autumn.

Less widely grown are two deciduous shrubby honeysuckles, *Lonicera tartarica,* which forms a large rambling bush, 3 metres high, bearing pink flowers in late May and early June, and *Lonicera fragrantissima,* which produces sweetly scented creamy white flowers in February. The last mentioned is best given the shelter of a wall or fence to protect the early flowers.

All the *Loniceras* are easy to grow and are not demanding in regard to soil.

Any pruning of the flowering types for shape should be carried out after flowering. Young hedge plants, set 25 cm. apart, need cutting back by half after planting and subsequent clipping is best undertaken in May and September. To ensure that hedges remain thick at the base and well furnished overall, the young growth should be cut back by one half every year until it reaches the desired height.

Lonicera pileata

Lonicera nitida

Lonicera nitida 'Baggessen's Gold'

MAGNOLIA

MAGNOLIA

Magnolia x soulangiana

Magnolia liliiflora 'Nigra'

Magnolia stellata

Magnolia sieboldii

Magnolia x soulangiana 'Nigra'

Most people are familiar with the dramatic, April-flowering *Magnolias*, shrubs and small trees with large, upright tulip-shaped flowers. Most common are forms of *Magnolia x soulangiana*, which bear an abundance of showy white flowers, suffused wine-purple outside, on leafless branches. *M. x s.* 'Picture' is a good modern hybrid similar to the type but flowering earlier. *M. x s.* 'Alexandrina' has the additional embellishment of a stronger purple flush at the base of the petals, whereas *M. x s.* 'Lennei' has entirely rose-purple flowers, like over-sized tulips.

One of the parents of *M. x soulangiana*, *Magnolia liliiflora*, is especially suited to the smaller garden reaching in height only 3.5 m. Erect flowers like slender tulips open between late April and June and often continue throughout the summer. Even more compact growth and slightly larger flowers, deep purple in colour, are provided by *M. liliiflora* 'Nigra'. A real garden gem is the "Star Magnolia", *Magnolia stellata*, which grows more slowly, ultimately to reach 3 m. It is heavily laden with masses of starlike white blooms in March and April. This and all the spring flowering forms need planting where the early blooms are protected from cold winds and from swift thawing in early sunshine after frost, both of which cause the blooms to become bruised and browned.

Summer flowering *M. sieboldii* is less well known, perhaps because the pendent, cup-shaped flowers appear amongst the leaves. They are pleasantly lemon scented and have crimson stamens in a ring, which contrast with the pearl-white flowers. The flowers are followed by pink fruit, which open in October to expose the orange seeds.

Magnolia grandiflora is, by contrast, a large evergreen tree, growing 5–7 m. high and 5 m. or more across, with large, laurel-like leaves, glossy green above and reddish-brown and felted beneath. Its large, strongly lemon-scented flowers, 20 cm. or more across, appear from July to September. While usually planted against a wall, it is hardy in the open in the warmer parts of the country. *M. g.* 'Exmouth' is the best form.

Many *Magnolias* are lime haters and are best in reasonably rich, deep soils. Provided that drainage is good, they will tolerate heavy clay soils and withstand the dirt of towns and cities. Warm, sheltered sites and soils well supplied with organic material in the form of leaf mould or peat will give the best growth. Balled plants should be planted March/April and careful attention to watering, mulching and protection from cold winds after transplanting is recommended. A little extra attention at the outset, to get the young plants established, will be rewarded by many years of exotic flowers.

Magnolia stellata

Magnolia grandiflora

Magnolia x soulangiana 'Alexandrina'

MAHONIA

japonica

aquifolium

Mahonia aquifolium

Mahonia 'Charity'

Rich, shiny, evergreen foliage is a feature of *Mahonia aquifolium*, which provides, as a bonus, bronze and purple tints in cold autumn and winter weather. Massed yellow flower heads are produced in March and April. The slightly fragrant flowers are followed by purplish-blue berries. It grows to 1–1.2 metres high and 2–3 m. across. A denser shrub, more spined and retaining the rich green colour into the winter is *M. pinnata*. The foliage, flowers and berries are all widely used by the flower arranger.

Better known are *Mahonia japonica* and *Mahonia x media* clones such as *M. 'Charity'*, which have exquisitely scented flowers from December to February with a fra-

grance similar to that of Lily of the Valley. Some nurseries offer the less common *M. bealei*, similar to *M. japonica* but with more upright and shorter flower spikes. All are excellent evergreen garden plants.

The *Mahonias* are not fussy over soil and produce the most richly coloured foliage in soil which has been improved by the addition of leaf mould and peat. All will stand shade, especially *M. aquifolium*, which can be used as a low hedge, in shrub borders, for ground filling and to cover ground under trees. Several species take a season or so to settle down but require little attention once established. *Mahonia aquifolium* can be cut back hard in April to maintain low and lush green growth.

MALUS

Among the many different species and hybrids of "Flowering Crab Apples" there are a number of excellent garden plants. These naturally bushy trees are usually grafted and grown on a clean stem 1–2 m. high to form standard trees. Smothered in their springtime blossom in April and May, they are a most striking sight. Several have decorative purple foliage and most bear large numbers of small but highly ornamental fruits in the autumn. The larger fruit is suitable for making into jelly.

Flowering and fruiting Crabs

While it is possible to group the many different "Flowering Crabs" by leaf colour, origin and fruit size, I aim to do no more than select some of the popular varieties and list a few that are especially well suited to smaller gardens. The natural shrubby form is attractive but it takes up more space and for this reason *Malus* is usually grown on a clear trunk as a specimen standard tree.

Best known is *M*. 'John Downie' with typical white apple blossom in spring followed by heavy crops of comparatively large, orange-flushed red, oval fruit. An even better garden plant is *M*. 'Golden Hornet', a neat, compact tree with white flowers and small, bright yellow, round fruits which remain intact well into the winter. This tree is an excellent pollinator of dessert and culinary apples. Equally attractive are *M. x robusta* 'Red Siberian' and 'Yellow Siberian', their respective colours referring to the cherry-like fruits which are carried in clusters on long stalks.

From the numerous copper and bronze-green leaved types, including such well known names as *M*. 'Aldenhamensis', carmine flowers and reddish-purple fruits, *M*. 'Wisley Crab', strong growing with purplish flowers and large fruits, *M*. 'Lemoinei', purple-crimson flowers and purple-bronze fruit, and *M. x purpurea*, purple flowers and fruits, I would choose a more recent and probably the most worthwhile garden plant, *M*. 'Profusion'.

MALUS

Malus
'Golden Hornet'

Malus 'Profusion'

This has clusters of large wine-red flowers, each bloom being some 4 cm. across, followed by rich young shoots of coppery-crimson foliage. It grows 5–7 m. high and produces a head up to 5 m. across carrying masses of small oval, dark red fruit.

A recent introduction, *M.* 'Van Eseltine', is ideal for small gardens, having compact upright growth. It carries flowers 5 cm. across, semi-double and rose-pink opening to lighter pink in colour. For me the most spectacular in flower is *Malus floribunda*, the "Japanese Crab". One of the earliest to flower, the small partially weeping head is absolutely filled with crimson buds that open as pale pink to white flowers. Rich green foliage and less spectacular yellow fruits follow the flowers. Similar in colour but later in its production of flower clusters is *M.* 'Hillieri'.

Any well drained garden soil is suitable and the *Malus* are much more reliable on heavy soils than *Prunus*, the flowering cherries. They respond with more vigorous growth where the soil has been improved by organic matter such as well rotted manure and peat. The vigour and ultimate size will depend to a great extent on the root-stock used by the nurseryman. The moderately vigorous stocks like Malling II and Malling Merton 111 are most commonly used, producing trees 7–8 m. high.

Strong support by staking is needed for several years until the trees are well established. They are ideal plants to use as specimens in lawns and beds. In mixed borders of shrubs *Malus* can be used to add height and colour in spring and autumn.

Little regular pruning is necessary, apart from the removal of diseased, thin and straggly shoots in the winter. Black spots on the leaves and fruit

Malus 'Hillieri' grown as a shrub

Malus x robusta 'Red Siberian'   *Malus x atrosanguinea*

are caused by the disease Apple Scab, which can be controlled by spraying at fortnightly intervals with captan from bud burst to mid July. Greenfly and caterpillar also attack the leaves and young shoots.

NERIUM

Nerium oleander

This evergreen plant is probably the most tender subject we have selected and, apart from the Channel Islands and the mild oceanic climate found in the warmest South West coastal districts of Britain, will need some protection. Large trusses of flower are carried for such a long period, from June to October, that this plant merits consideration for growing in tubs to stand on the terrace and patio all summer. It requires a minimum winter temperature of 7°C (44°F) and for this reason tub grown specimens will need to be housed in the greenhouse and sun lounge through the winter. There are white, cream, pink and yellow flowered forms.

Growing from 3 to 5 m high, its size can be retained by pruning back the flowered shoots by half after flowering and cutting the side growths back to within 10 cm of the main branches. March is a good time to repot, using John Innes Potting Compost No. 2. The *Nerium* is propagated by taking cuttings of half ripe wood in June and July. Once rooted, the plants are potted on and carried through the winter under glass. They are planted outside preferably against a south facing wall in May.

OLEARIA

Two species commonly named "Daisy Bush" are widely used by gardeners. The first, "New Zealand Holly", *Olearia macrodonta*, is a strong growing shrub reaching 3 m., with leaves that are rich green on the top surface and silver-white on the underside. An excellent subject for screens and hedging, especially in coastal areas, *Olearia x haastii* is also the hardier of the two and withstands city dirt and grime. It has smaller oval leaves, mid green above and grey-white felt beneath. Both are evergreen and have daisy-like flowers in clusters, the first-mentioned in June and *O. x haastii* in July and August.

Any well drained soil and sunny site is suitable for them and they grow well in chalk. Very little pruning is necessary and any dead branches are best cut out in April. These plants are particularly useful in mixed borders, for covering banks in coastal areas and in the shelter of walls inland, as well as for hedges and screens.

Olearia macrodonta

OSMANTHUS

Osmanthus delavayi

Rich, dark evergreens leaves are the feature of *Osmanthus delavayi*, which forms a neat rounded shrub some 2 m. in height and spread. The leaves are a perfect foil for the clusters of white flowers, which look and smell like jasmine. Less well known is the holly-like *Osmanthus heterophyllus* (syn. *O. ilicifolius*), of which there are several cultivars with prickly leaves marked silver, yellow and purple. They grow slowly to 2–3 m. high and have clusters of small scented white flowers in the autumn.

They are not demanding as to soil and will grow happily in both sun and partial shade. Exposure to cold northern and easterly winds is better avoided. The first mentioned does best with the protection of a wall but is excellent also for mixed borders, especially where deep, glossy foliage is needed in winter to show off the colour of other plants. The latter makes excellent dense hedges and for this plants should be spaced at 0.5 m. apart.

Paeonia suffruticosa

PAEONIA

Paeonia suffruticosa shrub

It is difficult to imagine more spectacular flowers than those of the "Tree Paeonies". Most popular as garden plants are the cultivars of *Paeonia suffruticosa*, which grow to some 2 metres in size and produce flowers 15–20 cm. across in April and May. The large compound leaves are also attractive in their own right. Although otherwise completely hardy, the tender young shoots produced each spring are susceptible to late frost and protection is recommended for these on cold nights until they have hardened.

This is best done by covering them with sacking and similar material at night and until the frost has thawed in the morning.

Moist but well drained soil, in sunny and partially shaded situations, is the ideal and enrichment with well decayed manure and peat will encourage strong growth. Annual mulching with manure is also beneficial.

The cultivars, many of which have oriental names like *P. s.* 'Jitsugetsu Nishiki', a bright scarlet, are grafted and the graft union, where shoot and root are joined, should be covered by 6 cm. of soil when planting. They are best planted towards the front of mixed borders in groups and, in sheltered gardens and sites protected from early morning sun, as specimens.

All the pruning required is the removal of dead and damaged wood in March and April.

Perovskia atriplicifolia

PEROVSKIA

Deep blue flower spikes in late summer and grey-green leaves with the fragrance of sage are the qualities of *Perovskia atriplicifolia*, commonly called "Russian Sage". It grows 1.5 metres high and thrives in chalky soils and in coastal areas. *P. a.* 'Blue Spire' has violet-blue flowers. Any sunny and well drained soil is suitable. They are best treated like herbaceous plants, cutting back to 24 cm. or so in March.
Use to the front of mixed shrub borders and with herbaceous plants.

The hard lines of a stone wall broken by purple leaves of *Berberis thunbergii atropurpurea* and *Cornus*.

PHILADELPHUS

Wafts of heady fragrance on a mid-summer evening are the hallmark of the white flowering *Philadelphus*, commonly called "Mock Orange", because of the similarity of its scent to orange blossom. Almost the perfect garden plant, being easy to grow, undemanding culturally, available in a range of varieties from 1–4 m., and very free flowering. By far the most popular is *P.* 'Virginal' which grows to 3 m. but is fairly upright, spreading little more than 2 m. It has large double flowers 25 cm. across, which are strongly scented and hang on the plant in clusters.

One of the best singles is *P.* 'Belle Etoile', growing 3 m. in height and spread. The base of the petals is flushed purple and the flowers are 5 cm. across and sweetly scented. A smaller shrub with even larger flowers is *P.* 'Beauclerc'. Of similar size but with denser growth and yellowish-white flowers is the widely planted *P. coronarius*. Little more than 1 m. in height and spread is *P. coronarius* 'Aureus', which has yellow leaves in spring turning greenish-yellow later in the season.

For the small garden and where the most compact forms are required the choice is twofold. *P.* 'Manteau d'Hermine' is a charming and very free flowering creamy-white, and *P. microphyllus,* with small leaves and fine bushy growth is covered densely with sweetly scented flowers. Both grow 1 m. high and little more than 1 m. in width.

Any garden soil is suitable and species of *Philadelphus* thrive in the poorest conditions, including chalk. Free draining soils are best and although they can be planted in partial shade, flowering will be better in more sunny situations. They are excellent plants for mixed borders, for screening and for planting schemes designed to provide fragrance.

The small-leaved *P. microphyllus* can be used at the back of rockeries. Little pruning is needed apart from thinning out old wood after flowering.

Philadelphus coronarius   *Philadelphus* 'Virginal'

Philadelphus 'Belle Etoile'

PHILLYREA

This dome-shaped evergreen has most attractive, narrow and glossy green leaves. Like a darker green and more refined laurel, *Phillyrea decora* (syn. *P. vilmoriniana*), produces small fragrant white flowers in May and purple-black fruits in the autumn. It is easy to grow and a plant worthy of greater use where an attractive evergreen cover is required. In mixed borders the rich foliage is very attractive in winter and an excellent foil to the red-barked *Cornus*. With no pruning required, the natural shape is wider than its ultimate height of 2 m.

Phillyrea decora

PIERIS

Pieris formosa forrestii 'Wakehurst'

Pieris japonica

Pieris 'Forest Flame'

Pieris (syn. *Andromeda*) is rapidly gaining in popularity as the forms whose young shoots are bright scarlet in spring become better known.

A neat, compact habit and attractive dark evergreen leaves make this genus well suited to the modern garden. Attractive red flower buds are formed in the autumn and open to white flowers, rather like arching flower stems of Lily-of-the-Valley, in April. They are slow growing and reach little more than 2 metres in height and spread after several years.

The hardiest and perhaps least attractive in leaf is *P. floribunda*. For the addition of copper coloured young shoots and larger but fewer flowers, *P. japonica* should be selected. The cultivar *P.j.* 'Variegata' is smaller and especially attractive, with small creamy-white edges to the green leaves, the young shoots are tinged pink.

For the greatest colour impact of bright scarlet shoots in spring *Pieris formosa forrestii* and the better clone *P.f.f.* 'Wakehurst' should be selected. These tender shoots can be damaged by spring frost, however, and a site which is sheltered and protected from the swift thawing of early morning sun is needed. A hardier hybrid *P.* 'Forest Flame' is rapidly becoming the most popular of all, its brilliant red leaves changing with age to pink, cream and then green.

Similar to *Rhododendrons*, these plants require lime-free soils and beds made up with acid peat are ideal. They grow best if not allowed to dry out and a mulch in spring with either leaf mould or peat helps. The only pruning required is the removal of dead flowers.

Excellent plants for mixed borders of heathers, *Rhododendron* and other lime-hating subjects, *Pieris* is attractive all the year round and can also be used as specimens, both singly and in groups.

Potentilla fruticosa 'Jackman's Variety'

POTENTILLA

There is no better group of plants for flower power than forms of the shrubby *Potentilla*, producing single rose-like flowers continually from June to the first frost. There are two broad groups, the taller, ideal for shrub borders and hedges and the low-growing types used increasingly for ground cover. Taking the more prostrate ones first, a good selection includes: *Potentilla arbuscula*, mid-green leaves and brown hairs identify this plant, which produces an abundance of large deep yellow flowers; *P. arbuscula* 'Beesii' has small yellow flowers carried against a background of silver-green foliage; often incorrectly listed as *P. arbuscula* is *Potentilla* 'Elizabeth', which grows in height and spread to 1 m., with bright yellow flowers; *P. fruticosa* 'Sunset' has a neat bushy habit with glowing orange flowers; *P.f.* 'Tangerine', the flowers of which are copper coloured in partial shade but yellow in full sun; and *P.f. mandshurica*, which has white flowers carried over silver-grey foliage. The most popular taller growing kinds, 1 m. and over, are cultivars of *Potentilla fruticosa*. There are a large number to choose from and my selection is; *P.f.* 'Jackman's Variety', a strongly growing shrub to 1.5 m. with large, rich yellow flowers; *P.f.* 'Katherine Dykes' grows to 2 m. and has rich yellow flowers; *P. fruticosa* 'Longacre', a plant spreading widely to over 1.5 m. with large canary-yellow flowers; and *P.f.* 'Veitchii' with pure white flowers.

All are very easy to grow in any garden but the best results are obtained on lighter, well drained soil. The best flowering occurs on plants in full sun, although partial shade is tolerated. No regular pruning is necessary but vigour will be maintained if old and weak branches are cut back to ground level in spring.

Apart from their use in mixed shrubberies, as low hedges and for ground covering, cultivars of *Potentilla* are excellent for the back of rockeries, on sunny banks and in dry, sunny sites close to walls.

Potentilla fruticosa 'Veitchii'

Potentilla fruticosa 'Sunset'

103

PRUNUS

for Hedging
the Laurels and flowering Plums.

Prunus laurocerasus

The "Common Laurel", *Prunus lauro-cerasus,* is one of the most widely used broad leaved evergreens for hedging, screening and shelter belts. Left unpruned it forms a large spreading shrub over 5 m. in height. The rich, shiny, light green leaves are most attractive, not only in the garden but also when cut.

It produces 'candles' of small white flowers in April, followed by red berries that turn black as they ripen. There are several cultivars with specific garden uses, for example, *P.l.* 'Otto Luyken', a more compact plant growing little more than 1 m. high, which is used extensively for ground cover planting. Even more prostrate and with willow-shaped leaves is *P.l.* 'Zabeliana'. Not commonly listed but of more upright form and with larger, more slender leaves is *P.l.* 'Caucasica'

Where slightly less coarse and gross leaf is required, *P. lusitanica,* the "Portugal Laurel", should be chosen. Darker green and with reddish leaf stems, it is one of the hardiest and will tolerate chalk better than cultivars of the common laurel.

When planting for hedges and screens, the plants should be spaced 70 cm. to 1 m. apart. Plants 1 m. and more high should be pruned back by one third after planting to encourage bushy growth and leaf cover from the base.

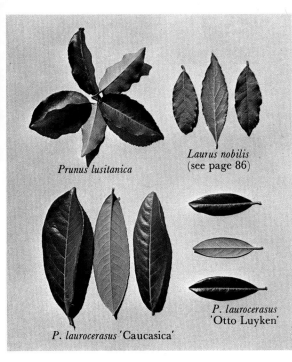

Prunus lusitanica

Laurus nobilis
(see page 86)

P. laurocerasus 'Caucasica'

P. laurocerasus
'Otto Luyken'

Prunus laurocerasus 'Otto Luyken'

There are three deciduous flowering "Plums" which make very attractive hedges. The lower growing *Prunus* 'Cistena', commonly called "Crimson Dwarf", produces rich copper foliage after the blush-pink star-like flowers in April. This is an excellent plant for edging, to form low hedges to 1.5 m. for formal beds and for underplanting among roses to strengthen their colour in summer. Plants can, if necessary, be clipped regularly and then old wood cut out in April to rejuvenate the plants and promote vigorous, richly coloured young growth.

Stronger growing, to 5 m. in height, is *P. cerasifera*, commonly called either "Myrobalan" or "Cherry Plum", and its cultivars. Left unpruned, *P. cerasifera* forms a small bushy tree, which has rich green wood, very early tiny white flowers and rich green leaves. The East Malling rootstock Myrobalan 'B' is a clone widely used for hedging under the common name "Greenglow".

Equally popular for hedging is *P. cerasifera* 'Pissardii', commonly called "Purple Flash". It has dark red bark and rich dark red young foliage that turns almost black with age. An attractive hedging combination is made by planting in sequence four Purple Flash and two Greenglow. These hedging subjects are best planted 36 cm. apart and pruned hard after flowering to limit their size and encourage their brightly coloured young foliage.

Prunus 'Cistena'

Prunus cerasifera 'Pissardii'

PRUNUS

Prunus 'Kiku-shidare Sakura'

for shrubs and small trees

the flowering Almonds, Cherries and

Peaches

One of the smallest flowering shrubs in this genus is *Prunus tenella*, the "Dwarf Russian Almond". It has thin willow-like leaves on arching branches reaching little over 1 m. in height and spread. The rose-pink, single flowers, 1 cm. across, smother the branches ahead of the leaves in April. *Prunus tenella* 'Fire Hill' is an excellent cultivar with rosy-crimson flowers.

A taller growing almond, sometimes grown on a stem to form a very small tree, is *Prunus triloba*. One of the earliest to flower, fully double rosetted flowers 2 cm. across are produced along the length of the slender stems in March and April. The flowers are produced on one-year old wood and hard pruning after flowering will encourage more growth and flowers twelve months later. An excellent plant for forcing, the stems can be cut in January and February to open indoors in water.

Another small shrubby almond is *P. glandulosa* 'Albiplena' which grows just over 1 m. in height and spread. The slender branches are weighed down with the clusters of fully double white flowers in April. It is best planted in a sheltered sunny site.

Flowering peaches are represented by *Prunus persica*, a species with comparatively few cultivars. They flower a little later than the almonds and in colours ranging from white to pink and crimson. *P.p.* 'Klara Mayer' is a popular small tree with bright double pink flowers.

Flowering cherries are perhaps the most popular of all small garden trees grown as standards or to branch from the base like a shrub. Especially well suited to the smaller garden are two "Japanese Cherries", *P.* 'Amanogawa' (syn. *P. serrulata erecta*) which grows upright just like a miniature "Lombardy Poplar" and the weeping form, which must be grown on a stem, *P.* 'Kiku-shidare Sakura', often sold under the name "Cheal's Weeping Cherry".

One other cherry which can be included in the tall shrub class is the March-flowering *P. subhirtella*. The most popular garden cultivar is *P. subhirtella* 'Autumnalis', which in contrast produces clusters of small, semi-double white flowers at intervals from November to March.

Almost all garden soils are suitable, if free draining, and those on the alkaline side are suitable for all but the common laurel. Apart from hedges and *P. triloba*, little regular pruning is necessary. Hedges of evergreen laurels should be pruned and trimmed with secateurs, not shears, to prevent halving leaves, and the best time for this is March/April and August.

Sparrows and Bullfinches damage the buds of several flowering *Prunus* and black cotton threaded through the branches deters their attack.

Prunus 'Amanogawa'

Prunus glandulosa 'Albiplena'

Prunus triloba

PYRACANTHA

Pyracantha in flower

Pyracantha coccinea 'Lalandei'

Pyracantha 'Orange Charmer'

Pyracantha 'Orange Glow'

Pyracantha atalantioides

The "Firethorns" have so many uses in gardens and for public landscaping that very extensive plantings are being made. Fortunately improved cultivars have recently been introduced which provide sheets of flower and sumptuous clusters of berries year after year. The best, in my opinion, is *Pyracantha* 'Orange Glow', a strong and fairly upright plant which has branches absolutely covered in orange-red fruit well into the winter. One of the good old ones is *Pyracantha atalantioides* (syn. *P. gibbsii*), which has very dark green leaves and produces large clusters of plump crimson fruit. The yellow-berried *P.a.* 'Aurea' has somewhat smaller fruit.

Best known of the older cultivars is the vigorous and upright *Pyracantha coccinea* 'Lalandei'. It bears clusters of medium-sized berries through the autumn and early winter. Two more to complete my selection: *Pyracantha* 'Orange Charmer' has dense clusters of orange fruits, and *Pyracantha rogersiana* 'Flava' has small but numerous clear yellow fruits.

Plants need to be pot or container grown for successful transplanting. All garden soils, including chalk, are suitable and forms of *Pyracantha* thrive in both sun and partial shade. The fierce thorns help to create impenetrable hedges, screens and barriers and protect the plants from vandalism. For hedges the spacing should be 60 cm. apart.

By far their most popular use is for furnishing walls and fences, even those facing north. Free standing, they reach 4 m. in height and spread but with the support of a wall they may reach 5 m. or more. Any pruning for shape should be carried out in May and June.

109

FLOWERS FROM SHRUBS ALL THE YEAR

Legend:

- ■ DECIDUOUS
- ◣ SOME DECIDUOUS SOME EVERGREEN
- ■ EVERGREEN
- □ WHITE FLOWERS
- YELLOW FLOWERS
- ORANGE FLOWERS
- RED FLOWERS
- PINK FLOWERS
- MAUVE FLOWERS
- BLUE FLOWERS

	JAN	FEB	MAR	APR	MAY	JUN	JUL	AUG	SEP	OCT	NOV	DEC
Amelanchier				■	■							
Azalea				■	■	■						
Berberis				■	■	■						
Chimonanthus	■	■										■
Camellia			■	■	■	■						
Carpenteria							■	■				
Caryopteris								■	■	■		
Ceanothus					■	■						
Ceanothus							■	■	■	■		
Cercis					■							
Chaenomeles			■	■	■							
Choisya					■	■						
Clerodendrum								■	■			
Cytisus					■	■						
Daphne		■	■									
Deutzia					■	■						
Erica/Calluna	■	■	■	■	■	■	■	■	■	■	■	■
Escallonia						■	■	■	■			
Forsythia			■	■								
Fuchsia							■	■	■	■		
Hamamelis	■	■										■
Hibiscus								■	■	■		
Hydrangea							■	■	■	■		
Hypericum							■	■	■	■		
Jasminum nud.	■	■	■								■	■
Jasminum off.						■	■	■	■			
Kalmia						■						
Kerria				■	■							
Kolkwitzia					■	■						
Laburnum					■	■						
Magnolia			■	■								
Magnolia						■	■	■				
Mahonia		■	■	■								
Malus				■	■							
Philadelphus						■	■					
Potentilla						■	■	■	■	■		
Prunus	■	■	■	■							■	■
Rhododendron				■	■	■						
Ribes			■	■	■							
Rosa						■	■	■	■			
Spartium						■	■	■				
Spiraea					■	■	■	■	■			
Syringa					■	■						
Tamarix					■	■	■	■	■			
Weigela					■	■						

Rhododendron catawbiense 'Grandiflorum'

RHODODENDRON

Many of the hardy hybrid cultivars of *Rhododendron* that grace the gardens of today were raised from *R. catawbiense*. There are innumerable species and cultivars, but there is space only to mention here some of the most popular. Breeders are currently introducing dwarf hybrids with larger and more colourful flowers, which are specially suited to the smaller garden.

Rhododendron 'Cynthia' (foreground)

Extensive woodland with broad walks lined with noble oaks is perhaps the perfect setting for banks of the stately, large-flowered *Rhododendron* cultivars. They can also play a colourful part in gardens of modest size. Some, like *Rhododendron* 'Pink Pearl', may in time outgrow a limited space and become bare at the base. They can be rejuvenated by cutting the branches hard back in April.

Most nurserymen list a number of cultivars in a good range of colour. Examples which immediately come to mind are: *R.* 'Britannia', a brilliant scarlet of low growing, spreading habit, reaching little more than 2 m. high; *R.* 'Gomer Waterer', white flushed pale lilac; *R.* 'Fastuosum Flore Pleno', semi-double lavender with dark crimson markings; and *R.* 'Sappho', white with a dark purple blotch.

For smaller borders and gardens, the dwarf forms must be considered. The heather garden and rockery are alternative sites for these delightful plants. There are true species like *R. impeditum*, which forms a very small mound 15 cm. or so high covered with pale mauve flowers in April; *R. williamsianum*, up to 1 m. high and 1.5 m. spread, producing bell-shaped flowers, red in bud paling to soft pink as they open; *R. lutescens*, growing to 3 m. with pale yellow flowers, slender willow-like leaves and, in common with *R. williamsianum*, glossy bronze young foliage.

Amongst the blue and lavender hybrids are to be found some of the most compact forms of *Rhododendron*. Such hybrids as *R.* 'Blue Diamond' and *R.* 'Blue Tit' have flowers which open pale lavender and intensify in colour as they age. Brighter in colour are the hybrids with bell-shaped flowers, typified by *R.* 'Elisabeth Hobbie', blood-red flowers; *R.* 'Elizabeth', bright scarlet; *R.* 'Bow Bells', silvery-pink; and *R.* 'Humming Bird', rosy red.

All members of the genus Rhododendron demand acid soil and where the ideal conditions do not occur naturally it is well worth creating them artificially. A well drained, chalk-free, sandy loam enriched with such organic matter as well rotted leaves, bracken, manure and peat is best. Any traces of lime and chalk will quickly turn the leaves pale and yellow.

This chlorosis can be overcome by repeated watering with Sequestrene. Heavy applications of Flowers of Sulphur, 100 to 150 gm. to the square metre, or heavy enrichment with peat will reduce alkalinity on marginal soils. The construction of beds, above the drainage water level and filled with peat, is the alternative. Be sure the plants never lack moisture, leaves curling backwards is a sign of dryness at the root, and for this reason sheltered semi-shaded sites are best. *Rhododendron* cultivars will stand full sun but regular mulching is recommended to keep these surface rooting plants happy. This same fibrous surface rooting allows easy transplanting and large specimens can be moved with success.

The only pruning necessary is the removal of dead flowers. This prevents seed heads forming and encourages the growth of next year's flower buds. It is best done by snapping out with finger and thumb. Flower buds which turn grey and brown in winter and develop black, bristle-like growths in spring are infected by the disease Rhododendron Bud Blast. They should be removed and burnt to prevent spread. Spraying in August and September with malathion will control rhododendron leaf hopper, whose attack encourages the spread of this disease.

Dwarf *Rhododendron* 'Elisabeth Hobbie'

Rhododendron 'Pink Pearl'

Rhododendron 'Doncaster' (foreground)

RHUS

Rhus typhina 'Laciniata'

Rhus typhina

Rhus glabra

Another plant too often dismissed because of its ease of culture and good nature is *Rhus*, commonly called "Sumach". Two species, *Rhus typhina* and *Rhus glabra*, are especially useful shrubs, the latter distinguished by a lack of dense hairs on the young shoots and its smaller ultimate size. Both have a cultivar called 'Laciniata', which has deeply cut, fern-like leaves.

The "Smooth Sumach", *Rhus glabra*, will reach 3 m. in height and 2 m. spread, the female plants producing conical light red flower clusters 12 cm. high in July, followed by dark red seed pods.

The larger "Stag's Horn Sumach", *Rhus typhina*, grows to 5 m. in height and spread and is by far the most commonly found in gardens. Densely packed, cone-shaped flowers 16 cm. long are also produced in June and July on the female plants, followed again by crimson seed heads. Male plants have a smaller, green flower spike. This species withstands the dirt and grime of cities and similar atmospheric pollution and if cut hard back in February produces vigorous young shoots with attractive leaves quite 36 cm. long. It has a tendency to produce suckers around its base and these can be invasive and a nuisance in small gardens.

All these plants have brightly coloured autumn foliage, the leaves turning from rich green to yellow-orange and red. Any ordinary garden soil is suitable and a sunny site will produce the most attractive leaf colour.

Pruning is not essential but cutting hard back every February, or alternate Februarys, will produce strong young growth and really sumptuous leaves. *Rhus* can be used as a specimen, either in grass or in cultivated beds, and in mixed shrub borders and for screening. This screening lasts only for the summer months and after leaf fall the typical Stag's Horn appearance of the branches will be seen.

RIBES

Ribes sanguineum 'King Edward VII'   *Ribes sanguineum*

Perhaps some of the most common flowering shrubs in gardens are the cultivars of "Flowering Currant", *Ribes sanguineum* is the best known species. They grow to 3 m. in height and 2 m. spread with clusters of colourful flowers hanging from the branches in March and April. Flowers of the type species are deep rose pink, *R.s.* 'King Edward VII' is a more compact plant and, like *R.s.* 'Pulborough Scarlet', has deep crimson flowers.

Less common is *Ribes odoratum*, the "Buffalo Currant", often sold incorrectly as *Ribes aureum*. This has bright yellow flowers in April which are, to me, most attractively scented. The shiny green leaves turn yellow and orange before falling in the autumn. Very occasionally listed by nurserymen is the hybrid, between the two species, *Ribes x gordonianum*, a very hardy and compact plant whose flowers are red on the outer edges and yellowish in the centre.

All grow well in ordinary garden soil and in both full sun and partial shade. The flowering is more colourful and more profuse in sunny sites. Pruning out old wood after flowering keeps the shrubs growing vigorously and provides plenty of the one-year old wood on which the largest flower clusters are produced.

While *Ribes* is mostly used in mixed shrub borders, the *R. sanguineum* cultivars make excellent hedges. Branches can be cut in February and March to flower indoors in water but the cut stems give off the characteristic currant smell usually connected with the fruiting blackcurrant, a close relative.

ROSA

There are very many excellent books, some of considerable length, which describe in detail the qualities of England's national flower, the rose. Here I can do no more than whet your appetite for the many quite delightful shrub roses. Left to grow with naturally arching branches, like wild "Dog Rose" under gentle restraint, they are a real joy in many garden situations.

There are so many from which to choose, from species and old cultivars to the latest introductions. The "Cabbage Roses", *Rosa centifolia*, include *R.c.* 'Cristata', the "Crested Moss Rose" and *R.c.* 'Muscosa', the "Moss Rose", popular with gardeners and painters since the 18th century. The richly scented flowers of the "Damask Rose", *Rosa damascena*, thought to have been brought to Europe by the crusaders in the 16th century, are used to make the fragrant oil Attar of Roses.

Early flowering yellow shrub roses are well represented by *R. x cantabrigiensis* and *R.* 'Canary Bird', which makes an excellent weeping standard. Both have delicately divided fern-like leaves. The "China Rose", *Rosa chinensis*, is thought to be one of the most important ancestors of our

Rosa moyesii

Rosa 'Frühlingsgold'

garden hybrids. The cultivar *R.c.* 'Cecile Brunner', the "Sweetheart Rose", is a favourite of mine, producing perfect, finger nail-sized pink buds in profusion.

The "Hybrid Musk" roses are renowned for their characteristic fragrance and several good cultivars are commonly listed by nurserymen, including *R.* 'Cornelia', a pale copper fading to pink, *R.* 'Felicia', a rich silver pink, and *R.* 'Prosperity', white flushed gold flowers.

For really large crimson fruits, the well known *R. moyesii* should be chosen. Both the species and its more compact form *R.m.* 'Geranium' have bright crimson, single flowers 5 cm. across. Coloured foliage can be provided by *Rosa rubrifolia*, which produces rich purple stems and leaves, as well as purplish-pink flowers 5 cm. across.

While *Rosa rugosa* is perhaps better known as a stock for growing standards, it has another useful role to play as high ground cover in planting schemes. Already widely used for roadside planting in Germany and Denmark, it is now being planted increasingly in Britain. Two excellent cultivars are *R.r.* 'Blanc Double de Coubert', large semi-double white flowers, and *R.r.* 'Frau Dagmar Hastrop', rich crinkled green leaves and rose-pink flowers followed by large, rounded and plump, crimson coloured fruits.

Most spectacular in flower are the more recent hybrids which include: *R.* 'Bonn', orange-scarlet flowers, *R.* 'Frühlingsgold', large fragrant clear light-yellow flowers, and *R.* 'Nevada', creamy-white.

The shrub roses are easy to grow and not demanding in soil and cultural treatment. Any reasonably fertile garden soil will give excellent growth. In gardens free of perennial weeds, annual weeds can easily be controlled with an early spring application of Simazine and similar selective weedkillers. The occasional removal of old wood will encourage new growth and rejuvenate the plants, and this is best done in early spring. *R. rubrifolia* ist best cut hard back in spring if the richest foliage colour is required, at the expense of flowers.

Many can be cut for use in flower arrangements and they are also suitable for hedges, screens and barriers.

The thorns reduce damage by vandals in areas troubled in this way. They can be used to clothe banks, to make specimens, in isolated beds and in grass. Varying heights allow their use in any position in a mixed shrub border and a shrub rose border, which will need very little maintenance, can be an attractive and colourful feature.

Rosa rugosa

ROSMARINUS

Rosmarinus officinalis

The very popular aromatic shrub "Rosemary" makes a pair with "Old English Lavender". Both revel in a warm, sunny site and require light, free draining soil for the best results. When planted in cold positions and heavy wet soils *Rosmarinus officinalis* will be cut back by cold winters and cold winds. It grows up to 2 m. in height and very nearly 2 m. spread if allowed to grow unchecked.

There is no fear of this plant not succeeding in the majority of gardens when it has been cultivated in Britain for over 400 years. There are several selected clones, of which the upright growing *R.o.* 'Fastigiatus', also known as *R.o.* 'Miss Jessop's Variety' is recommended.

All plants have long, narrow, rather thick leaves dark green on the upper surface and powdery white beneath. When crushed these leaves produce the beautiful rosemary fragrance. Branches produced the previous season carry pale blue flowers along the length of the stem in early summer.

A good plant for the front of shrub borders, to grow in narrow borders close to walls and on the patio. The upright clone will make an attractive low hedge which requires the minimum of trimming after flowering.

SALIX

Salix alba 'Chermesina' (syn. *Salix alba* 'Britzensis')

Salix x smithiana

The species of "Willows" number in hundreds and include plants of both shrub and tree dimension.

Plants outside the true shrub definition, like the very popular "Weeping Willow" tree *Salix alba babylonica* and "Pussy Willow", *Salix caprea*, are purposely omitted. A near relative of the weeping willow, *Salix alba* 'Chermesina', is included because hard pruning every second year will keep it shrubby and produce the desirable bright coloured young wood. If you have a large garden and like willowy stems for cutting, well furnished with silver-grey catkins in spring, then spare a thought for the British native *Salix x smithiana*. An alternative, still large in size, for those people fascinated by the Japanese art of flower arrangement is *Salix sachalinensis* 'Sekka', which produces curiously twisted and flattened stems if pruned hard.

Far more in keeping with the majority of plants in this book and ideal for every garden, including those of smaller dimensions, are several small and prostrate willows. The perfect example is *Salix lanata*, the "Woolly Willow". Slow growing, it barely reaches 1 m. in height and has a spreading habit. Rich, felty, silver-green leaves are the perfect foil for the large upright catkins. Another slow growing and spreading plant is *Salix hastata* 'Wehrhahnii', the naked branches of which carry slender silver catkins that stand like stalagmites. More prostrate is *Salix repens argentea*, the slender creeping stem being covered by silvery-green leaves and yellow catkins in spring.

Any ordinary garden soil is suitable, including those which are moist and occasionally waterlogged.

Light, dry soils will need improving by incorporating large quantities of peat, leaf mould and the like to retain moisture. Little, if any, pruning is needed for the dwarf types, apart from the removal of dead wood. Hard cutting back is necessary for the coloured bark kinds. The "Woolly Willow" is a suitable plant for the rock garden and all the lower growing kinds can be used in mixed borders, on banks, beside pools and to cover ground where a planting scheme with little maintenance is required.

Salix sachalinensis 'Sekka' (syn. *S. s.* 'Setsuka')

Salix lanata, detail

Salix lanata form

SAMBUCUS

Sambucus racemosa 'Plumosa Aurea'

The "Common Elderberry", *Sambucus nigra*, is very vigorous and its flat white flowers and clusters of black fruit are often used to make wine. The golden-leaved form *S.n.* 'Aurea' is usually chosen for garden planting and is most valuable for furnishing shrub beds and borders quickly. It usually needs pruning severely in late winter to induce strong young shoots and colourful foliage. The flat heads of white flowers, which it bears in June, have a rather insipid scent. The leaves are sometimes greenish when they first open but brighten as summer advances.

There are also cultivars with finely cut leaves, of which the most aristocratic is *Sambucus racemosa* 'Plumosa Aurea', slightly less vigorous than *S. nigra* 'Aurea'. It grows 2 m. high and 1 m. across. All forms of elder thrive in ordinary garden soils and in most positions, though their foliage will become greenish in shade.

SENECIO

Senecio grèyi

A plant popular for its felty silver-white leaves is the shrubby *Senecio*, which develops into a low, spreading plant up to 1 m. high. It has become very popular for its foliage and bright yellow flowers. It is decorative both in shrub borders and when cut for use in flower arrangements. It is also a good seaside shrub.

This New Zealand member of the vast daisy family produces masses of yellow daisies in generous clusters in June. It is a matter of personal choice whether these are left and enjoyed or cut away so that they do not detract from the foliage effect.

The most commonly listed is *Senecio greyi*, the true form of which is not as hardy as the garden form, which is really a hybrid clone. This clone has also been sold as *Senecio laxifolius*, which in fact is rather similar though with smaller, thinner pointed leaves.

All these forms of *Senecio* are easily pleased, being happy in most soils and situations though, like most other silver-leaved plants, they are at their best in full sun. If *S. greyi* spreads beyond the allotted space, it can be pruned quite severely in spring and soon produces new growth. A perfect plant to use at the front of shrub borders and in sunny borders against walls.

SKIMMIA

Another neat, dwarf shrub is *Skimmia japonica*, which grows little more than 1 m. in height and spread to make a compact evergreen bush. It forms clusters of tiny scented white flowers in March and April. The form 'Rubella' has bright red flower buds which make it unusually decorative throughout the winter. Male plants flower more abundantly but the females produce generous clusters of brilliant red berries, the size of large peas, which remain on the bushes through the winter until April. To make sure of these decorative berries, plant either one bush of each sex together or one male to three females. The alternative is to plant the hermaphrodite form, *Skimmia reevesiana*. The most fragrant is the male *S.j.* 'Fragrans' and the best female, with large bunches of berries, is *S.j.* 'Foremanii'. *Skimmia* is valuable for front positions in a shrub border, for small scale plantings and for tubs. It grows on most soils, but prefers a sandy or peaty soil and dislikes chalk, which can induce chlorosis (leaf yellowing). Being of neat growth it rarely needs any pruning.

COLLECTION G. TRUFFAUT

Skimmia japonica 'Rubella'

SPARTIUM

Spartium junceum

The "Spanish Broom", *Spartium junceum*, is a close relative of *Cytisus*, though it is more vigorous.

Growing up to 3 m. high, it produces rush-like stems with very few leaves. Its large pea-like flowers are bright golden-yellow, fragrant and appear in May and June.

It is used in the same way as the brooms. Tolerant of a wide range of soils and growing conditions, it thrives best in full sun on a well-drained, sandy soil and does less well on chalk. It is a good seaside shrub. It resents transplanting and for this reason it is wise to plant pot-grown and container-grown stock.

Leggy plants and those which have become too tall can be cut back in spring or even in autumn as long as pruning is restricted to young wood. A trim in the autumn tends to encourage earlier flowering the following year and the removal of dead flowers prevents seed production and self-sown seedlings appearing in the garden.

SPIRAEA

*Spiraea
x bumalda
'Anthony Waterer'

Spiraea x billardii 'Triumphans'

Spiraea x arguta

Spiraea douglasii

The spring-flowering species of Spiraea has white flowers. They are small to medium sized shrubs with branching, twiggy growth and an abundance of small flowers tightly packed in clusters. Most prolific in flowering is *S. x arguta*; the arching sprays of white flowers on this plant in April and May no doubt explain the common name the "Bridal Wreath". The earliest to flower is *S. thunbergii* with its slender sword-shaped leaves, which are light green and carried from February to November on plants little more than 1 m. in height and spread.

Closer in appearance to *S. x arguta* and with similar maidenhair fern-like foliage is *S. x vanhouttei*, but this grows to 2 m. or more high and up to 2 m. across.

Spiraea x vanhouttei

This is an excellent plant to use for hedging and screening, with dense twiggy branches creating a barrier in the winter. *Spiraea prunifolia* (syn. *S.* 'Plena') has double white flowers and bright red leaves in autumn and grows 2 m. high.

The summer-flowering *Spiraea* species usually have pink or red flowers in clusters or spikes. Little more than 0.75 m. tall is *Spiraea x bumalda* 'Anthony Waterer', which bears large flat heads of carmine-pink flowers from June to September. Cut hard back in spring, the resultant vigorous young shoots are cream-tipped, edged pink and valued by flower arrangers. Even smaller and reaching little more than 24 cm. are *S. x bumalda* 'Nana' and *S. japonica* 'Bullata'. These dwarf shrubs, with their deep rose-red and bright pink flowers respectively, are suited to the rock garden. Bolder in growth is *S. x billardii* 'Triumphans' (syn. *S. menziesii* 'Triumphans'), whose shoots reach up to 2 m. and are crowned with purple-rose flower spikes between July and September. Of similar form but shorter and suckering more from the base is *Spiraea douglasii*, whose deep pink flowers are produced in June and July. This is a good subject for the rougher, wilder parts of a garden.

Spiraea x bumalda 'Anthony Waterer'

All these species are easy to grow, are not discerning as to soil type and are valuable for shrub beds and borders. The cultivar 'Anthony Waterer' is an excellent low-growing plant for general garden use and especially for low maintenance planting schemes.

For the spring-flowering types, a light pruning after flowering to limit size is the only pruning required.

For large flower spikes of the summer-flowering species, harder pruning in spring is necessary.

Spiraea x arguta

123

SYMPHORICARPOS

Symphoricarpos albus

Symphoricarpos x doorenbosii 'Magic Berry'

The "Snowberries" are suckering shrubs about 1.5 m. high, with slender stems and tiny, blush-white flowers between June and August. These are followed by bright, white berries, which hang on for many months.

Commonly found in Britain is *Symphoricarpos rivularis* (syn. *S. albus laevigatus*), which grows up to 2 m. high and carries white fruits.

Symphoricarpos albus, which bears snow-white fruits like marbles 1 cm. in diameter, is more widely planted than *S. orbiculatus*, which has small purple fruits only 4 mm. in diameter but carried in dense clusters. The fruits hang on the bushes until February.

By crossing several species, a number of fine cultivars of *S. x doorenbosii* have been developed with relatively large fruits. *S. x d.* 'Magic Berry' makes dwarf growth and has rose-pink fruits, *S. x d.* 'Mother of Pearl' has white fruits, tinged pink, and *S. x d.* 'White Hedge' grows erect and compact to form a natural hedge.

Snowberries grow away quickly and easily, becoming naturalised in some areas, and thrive in all soils and situations, even under trees. They are used in shrub borders or for furnishing the wilder parts of a garden and quickly fill watersides and banks, thanks to their suckering growth. Their brightly coloured berries bring winter interest to the garden and are sought after for indoor decoration.

SYRINGA

The natural form of *Syringa vulgaris* cultivars.

For cutting, for fragrance and for garden decoration there are few shrubs better than the "Common Lilac", that is *Syringa vulgaris* cultivars. They are among the most popular of garden shrubs, growing ultimately 4–5 m. high and producing great clusters of flowers in May. The terminal buds on each branch produce flower clusters in pairs or even fours in colours ranging from pure white and pink to purple, red, mauve, violet and lilac blue.

Most nurseries list both single and double-flowering cultivars and these are some of my favourites:

Single-flowered: *S.v.* 'Marechal Foch', carmine-rose, tinted mauve; *S.v.* 'Maud Notcutt', pure white with exceptionally large flowers that last well in water when cut; *S.v.* 'Souvenir de Louis Spaeth', deep purple and one of the best tried and most free flowering.

Double-flowered: *S.v.* 'Charles Joly', deep purple-red with dark foliage; *S.v.* 'Katherine Havemeyer', heady fragrance and deep purple flowers, fading with age to lilac-blue; *S.v.* 'Madame Lemoine', a large double white which rightly immortalises the surname of the nurseryman who raised all these excellent double lilacs, including *S.v.* 'Michel Buchner', a true lilac-blue.

The only drawback to these cultivars is their short spring flowering period. Taking an average season and including the earliest and latest flowering, late April to early June is the

SYRINGA *(continued)*

Syringa vulgaris 'Charles Joly'

Syringa vulgaris 'Madame Lemoine'

Syringa vulgaris 'Katherine Havemeyer'

Syringa vulgaris 'Michel Buchner'

Syringa reflexa

Syringa velutina (syn. *S. palibiniana*)

extent of their season. This can be extended well into June by planting the later flowering species like *Syringa reflexa*, with drooping, clear-pink flowers and *Syringa sweginzowii*, flesh-pink flowers, and its larger form *S.s.* 'Superba'.

Hybrids from the parent *Syringa reflexa*, usually called "Canadian Hybrids", also extend the season well into June with loosely hanging clusters of flowers. Recommended cultivars include the rose-pink *S. x josiflexa* 'Bellicent' and the purple-pink *S. x prestoniae* 'Isabella'.

There is even a lilac for the smaller garden and rockery, *Syringa velutina* (syn. *S. palibiniana*); slow growing, its fine branches eventually reach 2 m. in height and produce masses of pale lavender-pink, fragrant flowers.

All these plants are hardy and thrive in well cultivated garden soils, especially the more fertile ones, and are quite happy on chalk. Hungry plants, their masses of fibrous roots quickly impoverish poor soils. The best flowering occurs in full sun and the flowers on shaded plants are thinner and less impressive.

Cutting branches while they are in flower for indoor decoration is one good method of pruning. The flower buds are formed in the previous summer and pruning in winter will therefore reduce flowering. It is essential to carry out some hard pruning occasionally to cut out thin and unproductive wood and to encourage strong new growth, which produces the largest flower heads.

This should obviously be done immediately after flowering.

Many of the *S. vulgaris* cultivars are propagated by grafting and a watch should be kept for suckers coming from the base of the plant. If this occurs, they should be cut off, otherwise they will grow strongly and take over from the desired cultivar.

TAMARIX

Tamarix pentandra

Tamarix tetrandra

The "Tamarisks" form quite large shrubs and small trees, with delicate leaves. Masses of tiny pink flowers clustered in short spikes cascade from arching branches. The stronger is *Tamarix tetrandra*, reaching 4 m. and opening its light pink flowers ahead of the leaves in May. Later flowering, in July and August, and brighter pink are *Tamarix pentandra* and its even darker form *T.p.* 'Rubra'. They grow little over 3 m. in height and spread, even in ideal conditions.

These shrubs have a graceful habit of growth, which makes them attractive in a variety of garden positions, including mixed borders, as single specimens, informal hedges, beside buildings and walls and by the waterside. They are especially tolerant of salt spray and wind, which explains their extensive use in coastal planting schemes.

Delicate in appearance but tough in constitution, they are at home in a variety of soils and situations. Well drained and sunny sites are the most suitable. Quite hard pruning is acceptable. The early flowering species should be cut back after flowering, while *T. pentandra* is pruned in winter and early spring. In both cases up to two thirds of the current season's growth should be removed to encourage bushy and well furnished plants.

127

VIBURNUM

Viburnum x burkwoodii

Viburnum opulus 'Compactum' in fruit

There is such variety in the types of *Viburnum* that one could almost have a garden furnished with them alone. Broadly divided into deciduous and evergreen, they have either white flowers or white flowers flushed pink. Several have a delicious fragrance and others carry richly coloured fruits and brightly coloured autumn foliage.

The *deciduous* types can be divided again into summer and winter-to-early-spring flowering. The earliest to flower is *Viburnum farreri* (syn. *V. fragrans*), with small clusters of fragrant pink buds and white flowers on the naked branches from November to March. It grows fairly upright to 4 m. in height and 3 m. spread and the young leaves are rich bronze in colour. More flowers and stronger rose-pink colouring is provided by two clones of the hybrid *V. x bodnantense*, which has *V. farreri* as a parent. Both *V. x b.* 'Dawn' and *V. x b.* 'Deben' are excellent garden shrubs with flowers which will stand quite hard frost.

Flowering in April and May but with larger flower heads is *V. carlesii*, one of the most sweetly scented of all shrubs and one of the most popular. Slow growing, it eventually reaches 2 m. high and 1.5 m. in spread. There are two smaller hybrids with even larger flower heads, 6–8 cm. across, *V. x carlcephalum* and the more compact *V. x juddii*.

The "Snowball Bush", *Viburnum opulus* 'Sterile', is a well known summer-flowering shrub. It can be forced into flower early and the opening flowers are tinted green.

The wild species *V. opulus*, commonly called "Guelder Rose", can be seen in the hedgerows especially when the translucent scarlet berries colour in the autumn. The presence of plants in the wild revelling in moisture indicates the requirements of such cultivars as *V.o.* 'Sterile', the free-fruiting *V.o.* 'Compactum' and the golden-yellow fruiting *V.o.* 'Xanthocarpum'.

Even more showy than the snowball shrub is *V. plicatum* 'Lanarth' (see illustration inside back cover). Branches form tiers and each tier is laden with large, flat white flower heads in May and June.

The *evergreen* types are of equal value in the garden. Winter flowering *Viburnum tinus*, commonly called "Laurustinus", can be used as an excellent replacement for laurel. Apart from the bright pink buds and large white flower trusses produced through the winter, it forms an excellent informal hedge and screen, withstanding shade, cold, wind and a very wide range of soil types. It grows to 3 m. in height and 2 m. spread.

For an evergreen but larger equivalent to *V. carlesii*, select the hybrid *V. x burkwoodii*, whose sweetly scented flowers open in April and May. Finally, and predominantly for foliage effect, there are the low-growing, ground-covering *V. davidii*, which has inconspicuous whitish flowers in June followed by turquoise-blue berries, and the taller *V. rhytidophyllum*, growing over 3 m. high with large white flower heads in May/June and red fruits which turn black in the autumn. Both require planting in groups to ensure pollination and the production of berries.

Viburnum opulus 'Sterile'

Viburnum rhytidophyllum flowers and fruits

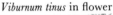

Viburnum tinus in flower

All species of *Viburnum* grow and flourish in a wide range of soil types. Well cultivated soils with sufficient organic matter to retain moisture are the ideal. Some species really thrive in chalk, for example *V. rhytidophyllum*, which can be used in such soils to provide the shape and form of *Rhododendron*. Pruning is not required, except perhaps to thin out old and damaged wood after flowering. Aphis can be a problem on some species, especially *V. carlesii* and the occasional spray to control this pest is recommended.

One or other of these plants can be used for nearly every purpose, for ground cover and screening, as specimen plants and to produce flowers for cutting. I strongly suggest considering a special border for *Viburnum* species; they would provide interest all the year round and, once planted, require little attention.

Viburnum carlesii

VITEX

Vitex agnus-castus

You need a very warm and sheltered south facing wall to grow *Vitex agnus-castus*. This plant demands free draining soil and plenty of sunshine to ripen the wood and produce the flower spikes. A spreading, aromatic shrub, it grows from 2 to 3 m high and the fragrant flower spikes are carried in September and October. It is not freely available in Britain. Prune in the spring by cutting back all last year's flowered shoots. The strong new growth will carry the new season's flowers.

WEIGELA

Weigela florida 'Variegata'

Weigela is widely planted and among the most popular shrubs, because of its easy nature and free-flowering habit. Still listed by some nurserymen under the generic name *Diervilla*, there are a number of excellent species and cultivars. I have selected some to make a representative collection. Firstly, *W. florida*, a strong growing plant reaching 2 m. in height and spread with rose-pink flowers in May and June. *W.f.* 'Foliis Purpureis', with dark purplish-green leaves and deep pink flowers, and *W.f.* 'Variegata', clear pink flowers and cream-edged leaves, are two compact, smaller growing cultivars that make excellent garden plants.

One of the most free-flowering is *W.* 'Bristol Ruby', with a fairly upright habit, up to 1.5 m. in height

Weigela 'Abel Carrière'

Weigela 'Eva Rathke'

Weigela 'Bristol Ruby'

and spread. The strong branches on this rounded shrub are covered with rich ruby-red flowers in May and June. For a shrub of similar size and shape and rose-pink flowers, *W*. 'Abel Carriere' should be chosen.

Well cultivated garden soil, preferably not too light and sandy, will give vigorous growth and full sun or partial shade are acceptable. In practice this means that all gardens can accommodate one or more of these colourful flowering plants. They can be used in mixed borders, against fences, to provide a low screen and to clothe banks.

Strong growth and plenty of large bright flowers will be maintained with quite hard pruning immediately after flowering.

YUCCA

The sharp, sword-shaped leaves of *Yucca* provide a complete contrast in form to most other shrubs and, for this reason, it is regularly featured in landscape architects' garden plans. The leaves of *Yucca filamentosa* spring from soil level in herbaceous form and reach no more than 75 cm. high. For a taller plant, *Yucca gloriosa* produces a short, thick trunk on top of which is the rosette of leaves reaching 2 m. Both produce large flower spikes up to 1 m. tall with cup-shaped flowers 6 cm. across. The former shrub flowers in July and August after two to three years' growth and the second in September and October after five years or so. The story that these plants grow, flower once and then die is a fallacy, as is the suggestion that they only flower once in every seven years.

Both are hardy in Britain and the most prolific flowering will occur in sunny sites and on well drained, sandy soils. They are best used as specimen plants and in conjunction with paving, the flat surface contrasting well with the sharp vertical leaves.

Yucca filamentosa

SHRUBS FOR NORTH WALLS	SHRUBS FOR SHADED SITES	SHRUBS FOR GROUND COVER
Camellia	Aucuba	Cotoneaster
Chaenomeles	Buxus	Cytisus
Garrya	Camellia	Erica
Kerria	Euonymus	Euonymus
Mahonia	Hedera	Genista
Pyracantha	Hypericum	Hedera
	Ilex	Hypericum
Climbers	Ligustrum	Lonicera
Hedera	Lonicera	Potentilla
Hydrangea	Mahonia	Vinca
Jasminum	Phillyrea	
Parthenocissus	Rhododendron	
	Skimmia	
	Vinca	

CLIMBING AND WALL SHRUBS

Clematis x jackmanii

Climbing plants are invaluable to present day gardening when it is often necessary to soften bleak concrete walls and to furnish hard brick surfaces. Smaller gardens and denser building result in a proliferation of fences and screens, all of which can be softened and made more decorative by the free use of climbers.

Campsis radicans
'Flava'

Campsis x tagliabuana
'Madame Galen'

CAMPSIS

The "Trumpet Vine", *Campsis radicans*, provides a less common and interesting alternative climbing plant, especially for pergolas, walls and fences. Both *C. radicans* and the hybrid *C. x tagliabuana* are hardy but need a warm sunny site to ripen the wood and provide a good show of flowers.

Given a warm site and rich soil, *Campsis radicans* will grow to 13 m and more and once established the self-clinging aerial roots hold the plant in position like ivy. The bright vermillion trumpet-shaped flowers 5–7 cm long are produced freely in August and September. *C. r.* 'Flava' has rich yellow flowers.

Hardier than the *C. grandiflora* parent, the hybrid *C. x t.* 'Madame Galen' is earlier flowering and has orange-scarlet flowers. All three illustrated plants are worthy of greater use, especially if the screens to be furnished have either a south or westerly aspect.

The flowers are produced on the current year's growth, so all plants can be pruned hard back in early spring. Newly transplanted specimens should be cut back to within 15 cm of the ground to encourage strong new basal growth. Large established specimens can also be cut hard back to rejuvenate them.

It is as well to tie in the young shoots and give them some support until they are re-established and self-supporting.

Campsis radicans

CLEMATIS

Large Flowered

Clematis 'Nelly Moser'

These pictures speak for themselves; it is not a matter of selecting cultivars and species but more a problem of deciding which to leave unmentioned. This selection includes old and well tried forms, as well as some more recently introduced cultivars. *Clematis* takes up little soil space and every garden would be improved by a good collection. The range of colour is indicated by the following:

'Duchess of Edinburgh'—large double white, fragrant, flowers May/June. Light pruning after flowering.

'Ernest Markham'—glowing carmine-red, flowers July to October. Prune hard in February.

'Hagley Hybrid'—shell-pink flowers June to September. Prune hard in February.

'Jackmanii Superba'—violet-purple, flowers July to September. Prune hard in February.

'Lasurstern'—large deep lavender-blue flowers June to October. Light pruning after flowering.

'Nelly Moser'—pale mauve-pink with carmine bar, flowers May to September. Light pruning after flowering.

'Hybrida Sieboldii'—pale blue-mauve, flowers May to September. Light pruning after flowering.

'Ville de Lyon'—deep crimson, flowers July/October. Prune hard in February.

'Vyvyan Pennell'—one of the best, fully double, deep violet-blue, flowers May to July. Light pruning after flowering.

Clematis 'Gypsy Queen'

Clematis 'Duchess of Edinburgh'

Clematis 'Vyvyan Pennell'

Clematis 'Ville de Lyon'

Pruning recommendations for the large flowered kinds can be made complicated. A simple practical method is to observe the flowering habit of the cultivar. Those which flower on the current year's growth should be pruned hard in early spring. The remainder, which flower on the previous season's growth, need only light pruning immediately after flowering. If the latter type become straggly and bare at the base, they too can be pruned back hard, again after flowering, to rejuvenate them completely.

Clematis 'The President'

Clematis montana rubens
close up of flowers.

Clematis alpina

Clematis orientalis

Small Flowered

Clematis montana as a screen

The species of *Clematis* with smaller flowers are generally much easier to establish, quicker growing and simpler to manage. The cultivars of *Clematis montana* are by far my favourite climbing plants, not only for their ease of cultivation and abundance of fragrant flowers in May, but also for their decorative seed heads. The foliage is retained well into the winter and makes the plants more effective for screening and covering unsightly sheds and fences. The true species *C. montana* grows rampantly to 10 m. with the support of old trees, fences and trellises.

In full flower the whole plant is a mass of white. *C.m. rubens* has rose-pink flowers which look well against the rich purple-bronze young shoots.

C.m. 'Tetrarose' has larger flowers, up to 8 cm. across. Pruning, if necessary to limit size, is best done after flowering.

Attractive silvery seed heads are borne by *Clematis orientalis,* commonly called the "Orange-peel Clematis" because the thick orange sepals curl back rather like the freshly cut peel of an orange. The fine, rapidly growing stems intertwine to 5 m. and the flowers are produced from August onwards. Very similar is *C. tangutica,* which starts flowering in July and also produces silky seed heads. They both respond to hard early spring pruning.

All *Clematis* require a rich moist soil which contains some chalk. It is wise to imitate as far as possible the conditions that suit the wild *Clematis,* a deep cool root run under hedges and thickets, the branches growing through the shrubby growth to revel in space, sun and air. In gardens the roots can be kept cool either by covering them with paving or by shading them with shrubs and herbaceous plants. The stems need the support of trellis or branches.

A good mulch with manure is recommended each spring to encourage vigorous growth.

HEDERA

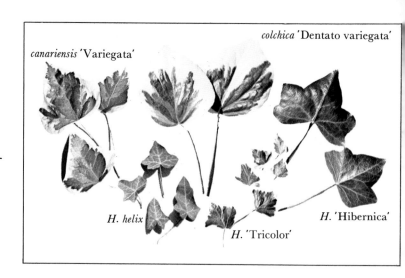

canariensis 'Variegata'

colchica 'Dentato variegata'

H. *helix*

H. 'Tricolor'

H. 'Hibernica'

Hedera colchica 'Dentato-Variegata'

Hedera helix 'Baltica'

Hedera canariensis 'Variegata' (syn. *H.c.* 'Gloire de Marengo')

The species and cultivars of "Ivy" are now serving a dual role in gardens. Increasing use is made of them for ground cover as well as in their well established use as climbers. There are few more attractive ways to cover a wall, fence or pillar than with plants of *Hedera canariensis* 'Variegata' or the even hardier *Hedera colchica* 'Dentata Variegata'. The hardier plant is more golden in colour, richer but not as fresh looking as the "Canary Island Ivy", which is also a popular house plant. If you prefer plain green leaves, then both the true *H. canariensis* and *H. colchica* will grow and cover more rapidly than the variegated forms.

The smaller-leaved *Hedera helix*, the "Common Ivy", is equally attractive for wall covering, and its cultivars *H.h.* 'Glacier' which has silvery-grey, white-edged leaves, as if covered in hoar-frost, and *H.h.* 'Gold Heart', whose leaves have a bold yellow centre, are more showy. All these may need some support until the aerial roots gain a hold.

When planted for ground cover nothing could be simpler. Vigorous young pot-grown plants spaced 24–30 cm. apart soon cover the soil with a verdant canopy. A number of cultivars including the rich green *H.h.* 'Baltica' are being used for this, in addition to the well established names.

Soil is no problem because ivies thrive in almost impossible situations, including dense shade, impoverished soil and in strong competition with other woody plants. Give them better conditions and the foliage will shine like the leaves of freshly polished house plants. For the strongest colour variegation of silvers and golds, plant in sunny sites.

Wall plants are best pruned back in early spring and straying shoots should be cut away from pipes and gutters in mid summer. Even the ground cover specimens benefit from a "short back and sides" every now and again.

HYDRANGEA

Hydrangea petiolaris is a hardy, self-supporting climber. Its attractive, glossy green leaves are especially attractive when seen covering walls and old tree trunks. Large white flower heads, rather similar to the Lacecap forms of *Hydrangea* and 12 cm. across cover established plants in June/July. This is an excellent plant for sunless north walls. It may need some support until the aerial roots grip whatever support is provided.

Given ample moisture and wall support, it can reach over 20 m. in height and spread. Free-standing shrubs do not grow as tall but are equally attractive.

Hydrangea petiolaris

JASMINUM

Jasminum officinale

The "Common White Jasmine", *Jasminum officinale*, is one of the stronger growing climbing plants. Given the support of an old tree trunk or trellis, it grows to 9 metres in height. Attractive dark green leaves are slow to fall and, as the branches are also dark green, an almost evergreen appearance results. Very fragrant, white flowers are carried in clusters from mid-summer to September. Vigorous leaf growth tends to hide the flowers and hard pruning aggravates this. A warm, sunny site is needed to encourage free flowering.

Slightly larger flowers and a pink tinge to the buds are provided by *Jasminum officinale* 'Affine' (syn. *J.o.* 'Grandiflorum').

Both the species and the improved form are excellent for screening and to furnish bare walls.

Little pruning is necessary, apart from the removal of any frost damaged shoots in spring. Any thinning of old growth and pruning to contain the plant should be done after flowering.

LONICERA

Lonicera periclymenum 'Serotina' climbing plant

The "Woodbine", our common hedgerow honeysuckle, *Lonicera periclymenum*, has a sweet and fresh fragrance all of its own. No country garden should be without this plant, whose pale yellow flowers open in July and August followed by clusters of translucent scarlet berries.

Of equal merit are the two cultivars most commonly listed by nurserymen, *L.p.* 'Belgica', "Early Dutch Honeysuckle", and the supposedly later flowering *L.p.* 'Serotina', "Late Dutch Honeysuckle".

Extension of the flowering season is more certain with other species like the less common *L. x brownii* 'Fuchsoides', a semi-evergreen with scarlet flowers from June to September, *L. x heckrotii*, flowering for a similar period, and *L. japonica*, a rampant growing plant to 10 m. which has very fragrant pale cream flowers in the axils of the leaves on the young shoots. The leaves of the "Japanese Honeysuckle" tend to hide the flowers and the golden netted and veined leaves of *L. japonica* 'Aureoreticulata' are a more reliable source of colour the year round. This is a plant sought after by flower arrangers and just as well suited to ground cover use as it is to climbing.

Similar conditions to those for *Clematis* are the ideal, rich, damp soil and shade at the root. The honeysuckles are not so dependent on sunshine for flowers, however, and partial shade suits them well. Plenty of leaf mould and mulching with peat encourages growth and flowers.

Regular pruning is not required and the occasional removal of old wood will be all that is needed.

While many climbing honeysuckles are planted against house walls, they grow better and look more attractive when given the freedom to scramble over arches, trellises and sheds. A study of old cottage gardens will soon reveal suitable sites, like the example illustrated on the back cover of this book.

japonica 'Chinensis'

Lonicera caprifolium

Lonicera periclymenum 'Serotina'
close up of flowers

Lonicera x heckrotii

Lonicera japonica 'Aureoreticulata' foliage plant

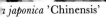

PARTHENOCISSUS

foliage of *Parthenocissus*
Autumn adult foliage colour

Parthenocissus tricuspidata

summer juvenile foliage

Parthenocissus quinquefolia

Much confusion surrounds the names of these vines, due perhaps to earlier references under the names *Ampelopsis* and *Vitis*. The confusion becomes greater with the common name "Virginia Creeper" sometimes being applied to the wrong plant.

The best known and most widely planted, especially against older suburban houses, is *Parthenocissus tricuspidata,* commonly called "Boston Ivy" and occasionally still listed as *Vitis inconstans*. A smaller-leaved form with young growth tinged purple is *P.t.* 'Veitchii'. With more deeply cut and five-lobed leaves is the true "Virginia Creeper", *Parthenocissus quinquefolia*. Most colourful of all is *P. henryana*, which has dark bronze-green leaves and if grown in shade, each mid rib shows white and pink variegation. All these species and cultivars turn rich scarlet in the autumn and are self-clinging to walls, fences, tree stumps and the like. Both *P. tricuspidata* and *P. quinquefolia* would furnish a telegraph pole, provided the leading shoots are kept clear of the lines.

The ideal rich loamy soil and plenty of moisture will give rapid growth, but acceptable results can be obtained in most gardens if the soil is well cultivated and enriched with organic matter before planting. Pruning need be no more than the removal of unwanted shoots in summer.

PASSIFLORA

The "Passion Flower" *Passiflora caerulea*, has exotic flowers opening from June to September. While not completely hardy, it will grow and flower in most gardens, given a warm south or westerly facing site.

The flowers are sometimes followed by large orange fruits. Similar, but with ivory-white flowers, is *P.c.* 'Constance Elliott'.

Given the warm site and a well drained soil, this plant will grow rapidly 7–10 m. high, supporting itself with tendrils. Pruning is best undertaken in spring and includes the removal of dead wood and cutting back to limit size. Cold winter weather will damage the upper growth but, if this is pruned away, strong new growth will spring from the base after all but the hardest of winters. If you want a climbing plant with flowers to challenge the orchid, make space for the passion flower.

Passiflora caerulea

POLYGONUM

Polygonum baldschuanicum

The common name "Mile-a-Minute" aptly describes the growth of *Polygonum baldschuanicum*, which is also known as the "Russian Vine". Once established, it can comfortably grow 5 m. in a year and is the perfect subject to cover rapidly eye-sores as bizarre as old air raid shelters, cars, garages, sheds and oil tanks supplying the heating system. The twining growth completely covers anything in its path and frothy, creamy-white flowers top the foliage from July to the first frost.

It is worth paying a little attention to soil if you require quick establishment, but any site and soil, including chalk, will support its rampant growth.

Pruning is hardly the word if the plant is allowed to develop out of hand, "Jungle warfare" in hacking back the superfluous growth in spring is a better description.

WISTERIA

Wisteria floribunda

Wisteria sinensis

The two most popular species are *Wisteria floribunda*, which has leaves with 13 to 19 oval leaflets and clockwise twining stems, and *Wisteria sinensis*, most leaves of which have eleven leaflets and the stems twine anti-clockwise. While identification is easy, there is little need to choose between them. Both are superb plants once established and an absolute joy in May, when the great trusses, 20 cm. long and more, of fragrant mauve flowers hang from the leafless branches. Both species have a white cultivar called 'Alba'.

Most spectacular of all is *W.f.* 'Macrobotrys' (syn. *W. multijuga*), which has the longest racemes of flowers.

They do not take kindly to root disturbance and for speedy establishment, container grown plants are recommended. If newly transplanted specimens are slow to break into growth, do not despair, an occasional spray with water will help speed shoot development.

In my experience *Wisteria* is not fussy when it comes to soil. Anything from heavy clay to quite light soil is acceptable but they thrive best on an ample supply of moisture. A sheltered site and the protection of a south or west facing wall prevents wind and late frost damaging the flowers. It is possible to train a single stem up to form a trunk and with regular pinching produce a free-standing tree with pendent flowers.

Pruning can be undertaken twice in the year. All lateral side growths from the main branches can be cut back to within 2–4 cm. of the flowering spurs in February and on very vigorous plants the current year's lateral growth can be shortened in August, before cutting hard back the following February. While there are a number of classic plant associations like *Wisteria* growing through *Laburnum*, and twining through rustic wood on a bridge over water, some of the most practical supports are arches and pergolas. If interplanted with climbing roses they extend the season of flower.

INDEX